Cambridge

THEN AND NOW

BATSFORD'S

Cambridge
THEN AND NOW

Vaughan Grylls

BATSFORD

First published in the United Kingdom in 2011 by
Batsford
10 Southcombe Street
London
W14 0RA

An imprint of Anova Books Company Ltd

ISBN: 978-1-84994-022-1

A CIP catalogue record for this book is available from the British Library.

16 15 14 13 12 11
10 9 8 7 6 5 4 3 2 1

Reproduction by Rival Colour Ltd, UK
Printed by 1010 Printing International Ltd, China

This book can be ordered direct from the publisher at the website: www.anovabooks.com

PHOTO CREDITS
The publisher wishes to thank the following for kindly providing photographs for this book:

All "Then" photographs are courtesy of Anova Image Library, except for the following:
Pages 12, 38, 40, 52, 54, 96, 106, 110, 114, 116, 118 courtesy of the Cambridgeshire Collection.
Pages 28, 48, 102, 104, 124, 126, 136, 140 courtesy of the Francis Frith Collection.
Page 128 courtesy of the Cambridge and County Folk Museum.
Page 130 courtesy of the author.
Page 134 courtesy of Murray Edwards College.

Thanks to Vaughan Grylls for taking all the "now" photography in this book.

Front and back covers show the Mathematical Bridge, Queens' College,
then (photo: Anova Image Library) and now (photo: Vaughan Grylls).
Pages 1 and 2 show Newnham College, then (photo: Francis Frith Collection)
and now (photo: Vaughan Grylls).

AUTHOR ACKNOWLEDGEMENTS

Writing *Cambridge Then and Now* was for me a very personal experience for I am part of its Then. As a student at University College London's Slade School of Fine Art, I had a summer job working for a company called Undergraduate Tours. Escorting tourists around Cambridge meant I got to know the city well. A few years later, my first full-time job was at Homerton College Cambridge where I taught sculpture from 1971 to 1973. I lodged near Hills Road with Mrs Waters, a retired headmistress who also happened to be the mother of Roger, the founding member of Pink Floyd. Although I eventually left Homerton to return full-time to my own work, for a decade I returned to the college once or twice a year as a visiting artist and on those occasions I always took pleasure in wandering round the city on my own. Yet the idea of producing a book on Cambridge based entirely on my own knowledge would have been foolish and so I am delighted that many people have been kind enough to help and advise me. It is to my chagrin that I cannot give sufficient credit to each in the space available here.

My first and foremost, acknowledgement is to my wife, Polly Powell, for suggesting this as an obvious companion to my book *Oxford Then and Now* (Batsford, 2009). Those following were equally helpful in various ways. Geoffrey Tyack, probably the world's leading authority on the architecture of Oxford, pointed me in the direction of Tim Rawle and his impressively detailed *Cambridge Architecture* (Andre Deutsch, 1985). Geoff, however, was unforgivably modest when he omitted to mention that he himself was the author of the excellent *Oxford & Cambridge* Blue Guide (A & C Black, 2004), the most readable yet authoritative handbook on the city. Benedict Le Vay's *Eccentric Cambridge* (Bradt, 2006) was always fun to turn to, while Martin Garrett's *Cambridge* (Signal, 2004) provided a rich cultural and historical background, consistently reaching places bypassed elsewhere. I experienced one or two *Cambridge Then and Now* moments myself in the relatively short time between taking the photographs and writing the captions. The Globe pub became the Emperor almost overnight, whilst the Cambridgeshire Collection, a wonderful archive and part of the Public Library, moved from the outskirts of the city to the Grand Arcade shopping centre. Luckily, when the photographs and other material moved so did all the people working there. I am indebted to Chris Jakes and his staff, particularly Sue Slack, Elizabeth Stares and Fiona Parish, for magically producing old photographs I had asked for, and for then suggesting much better ones. Where I had more gaps to fill, Sarah Brown, Collections Officer at the fascinating Cambridge & County Folk Museum, proved invaluably helpful. At Murray Edwards College, Kate Love produced a brilliant photograph of a suspended segment of Chamberlin, Powell and Bon's huge dome being craned into place.

Many of the 'Then' photographs of the colleges are by Eric de Maré or A.F. Kersting. My decision to choose their work over others was purely based on quality. Here were two architectural photographers whose expertise was evidently of a different order to that of most photographers today, including, I must admit, my own.

Posing for a photographer can often be a tiresome experience. I trust it was not too much of an ordeal for the students of Homerton College, who one Saturday morning, and very early for them as they said (it was an 11am call after all), gamely got out of bed to assemble on the lawns of their college for a 'pun-sculpture' in the exact place where their predecessors had done the same for me thirty-six years earlier. My thanks to the Principal of Homerton College, Dr Kate Pretty, CBE, for encouraging that particular reprise.

Last but not least are Frank Hopkinson and David Salmo, my editors at Anova Books. Having trained me thoroughly on *Oxford Then and Now*, their gentle nudging brought to this book whatever was needed and edited what wasn't.

Time is a gentler public judge of works of art, books or performances, for these can be secreted away to be appreciated anew as fashion demands. The same cannot be said for architecture, which, by its very nature, is always in the public domain. Where it fails the fashion test, it can be tinkered with or even destroyed. Thus I have the highest regard for architects as the bravest of those of us who call ourselves artists. Imagine today attempting to add a new college or major extension to Cambridge's illustrious architecture. It is therefore to those late twentieth-century practices who fearlessly ventured forward, such as Chamberlin Powell and Bonn, that I dedicate this book, remembering especially Geoffry Powell, my father-in-law.

A SHORT HISTORY OF CAMBRIDGE

The Renaissance scholar, Erasmus of Rotterdam, made some disparaging comments about Cambridge during his time at Queens' College. He implied that it wasn't up to scratch with Italy, which he had left in 1509 for Cambridge. No credit was given to King's College Chapel, even though he was there when its fan-vaulting was being completed. Perhaps, as a Renaissance man, he did not think this final flowering of medieval English architecture worth mentioning. Instead he complained about important matters such as food and drink, clearly beneath the standards expected by a man of the world.

Although there were settlements in the Cambridge area before the Romans – a 3,500-year-old farmstead discovered in the grounds of Fitzwilliam College, an Iron Age hill fort on Castle Hill – it was not until c. AD 70 with the arrival of the Via Devana, a military road, that a place to defend the crossing of the Cam was required. The crossing was near present-day Magdalene Bridge and the Roman name for it (like the later name, Cambridge) described precisely what it was: Duroliponte, the bridge over the Duro (the Celtic word for water).

After the Romans formally abandoned Britain in AD 410, Saxon settlers took over the site, naming it (according to the *Anglo-Saxon Chronicle*) Grantabrycge. The arrival of the Vikings, also recorded in the *Chronicle*, and the Danelaw in 878 made Cambridge of interest as it was as far up river as could easily be reached for trading. The Vikings settled on the left bank and the two communities may have traded with each other. During this period present-day Market Hill became established for trade, for although just a rise in the ground, it was high enough to avoid river flooding and it was close to the still-used Roman road. A town centre developed and it was from here that modern Cambridge grew. In the century before the Norman Conquest of 1066, the Saxons briefly returned to power, evidenced by the oldest structure in Cambridge, St Benet's Church, built in 1025.

In 1068 the Normans built a castle on Cambridge's only real hill. The Round Church was also built at the junction of the Roman road and a Saxon lane running between Market Hill and the wharves, where the grandest colleges now stand. Over time, the name Grantabrycge went through various mutations: Grentabrige, Cantebrigge, Cambridge. The Cam between Cambridge's Millpond and the village of Grantchester is still called the Granta. Cam is derived from the name Cambridge rather than the other way round. Later, Cambridge University coined the Latin term 'Cantabrigiensis' ('of Cambridge'). Contracted, this is still found in degree appellations – for example, MA (Cantab).

In 1209 violence between 'town and gown' erupted in Oxford, causing some scholars and students to flee. They settled in the market town of Cambridge and over time established patterns similar to Oxford. In 1231 the university at Cambridge received a charter from Henry III, giving it the right to discipline its members, as well as some tax exemptions. Two years later Pope Gregory IX issued a bull allowing Cambridge graduates to teach 'anywhere in Christendom'. In 1284 the first college, Peterhouse, was established, followed in 1317 by King's Hall and in 1324 by Michaelhouse (in 1546 these last two were subsumed into the new Trinity College.)

The increase in colleges, with endowments and influence, encroached on the market town and in 1445 busy wharves and whole streets were flattened to make way for King's College (a development difficult to imagine today as one gazes over the serene Backs). Clearances, if not on that scale, continued until the early twentieth century, for the colleges owned the freehold on many of the ordinary houses and commercial properties in Cambridge.

Founders and endowers of colleges normally asked scholars to pray for their souls in exchange for their donation. To help them do so colleges were often linked to religious houses. Such undemanding duties ceased with the Dissolution of the Monasteries in 1536 when Henry VIII provided perhaps the earliest, and certainly the most effective, example of political interference in an academic curriculum through ordering the university to cease teaching 'Canon Law' (the laws of the Church) and instead teach the Bible, the Classics and Mathematics. Using Thomas Cranmer (an alumnus of Jesus College) as his principal instrument, Henry set the stage for a peculiarly English version of the Protestant Reformation, one that cut a path between abhorrence of the Pope and suspicion of Martin Luther and other Continental Protestants.

Cambridge's Protestant contribution turned, in the following century, towards the greater extreme of Puritanism, most in evidence at Emmanuel, St Catharine's, Sidney Sussex and Christ's colleges. They produced many graduates, who argued that the so-called Church of England was sliding back towards Rome. Partly due to their influence, around 20,000 emigrants left England in the 1630s, seeking a 'new England' in Massachusetts. Cambridge's puritan explosion was to provide the matrix for many other events with far-reaching consequences, such as the establishment of the first university in the American colonies (John Harvard – Emmanuel) and the outbreak of a Civil War in England (Oliver Cromwell – Sidney Sussex), ending with the execution of the King and the establishment of a Commonwealth that anticipated modern Parliamentary democracy.

Religion and politics are not the only areas of influence. Cambridge has made a huge impact in mathematics and science. This can be traced back at least to Francis Bacon (Trinity College), a pioneer of 'scientific method' whose *Novum Organum* (1620) laid the ground for the centrality of empirical research. The young Bacon was a Puritan and it is interesting to note that the year of his book's publication was the same year the Pilgrim Fathers arrived in Massachusetts. In 1687 the scientific method reached its apogee in the publication by Sir Isaac Newton (Fellow of Trinity College, Cambridge and Lucasian Professor of Mathematics) of his *Mathematical Principles of Natural Philosophy* – the *Principia*. It is perhaps the greatest scientific book ever written. Newton's view of the universe would dominate world science for the next 250 years.

Cambridge's leadership in the sciences continued, as the following examples demonstrate: discovery of hydrogen (Henry Cavendish, 1766); invention of a proto-computer (Charles Babbage, 1822); publication of *The Origin of Species* (Charles Darwin, 1859); discovery of the electron (J.J. Thomson, 1897); 'splitting of the atom' (Ernest Rutherford, 1917); pioneering of quantum mechanics (Paul Dirac, 1930); 'splitting of the nucleus' (John Cockcroft and Ernest Walton, 1932); groundwork for the modern computer (Alan Turing, 1936); and the discovery of the double helix structure of DNA (Francis Crick and James Watson, 1953).

The greatest vehicle for promoting the Cambridge brand was the Cambridge University Press (CUP). With letters patent granted by Henry VIII in 1534, the CUP is the oldest continually operating book publisher and the oldest university press in the world. Alongside its scientific publications, it has published all the main editions of the Bible, starting in 1591 with a forerunner of the King James Version, the Geneva Bible. Other acclaimed publications include its Cambridge Histories and authoritative editions of Shakespeare. Today CUP produces print and online books that penetrate a global market. Its forte is educational publishing.

Cambridge as a city saw extensive building in the later nineteenth century. The arrival of the railway in the 1840s provided an impetus, since materials and equipment could then be moved more easily. New colleges (some, for the first time, open to women), and new civic and commercial buildings have all made their appearance, yet they have not changed the feel of Cambridge as fundamentally a market town.

In 1928 the Festival of Nine Lessons and Carols by the Choir of King's College Chapel was first transmitted on the radio. It is now a national tradition and the recordings are world famous.

The twentieth century saw suburban spread and after World War II, modernist architecture arrived, usually in the form of new colleges such as Churchill, New Hall (now Murray Edwards) and Robinson, or of major extensions such as Powell and Moya's Cripps Building for St John's. Outside the city, Cambridge Science Park emerged, reminding us that despite the town's largely antique appearance, it has for centuries provided a habitat for those who look forward.

In 1992 Cambridge gained its second university. Anglia Polytechnic would become Anglia Ruskin University after John Ruskin, who opened its forerunner, the Cambridge School of Art, in 1858.

Entertaining the public has not been confined to the Christmas broadcast from King's College Chapel. Several bands started in Cambridge, the most famous being Pink Floyd. Cambridge University's amateur dramatics club, the Footlights, was founded in 1883 and since the 1960s has been a nursery for satirists and stand-up comics. Those who became household names include Clive Anderson, David Baddiel, John Cleese, Peter Cook, David Frost, Stephen Fry, Tom Hollander, Clive James, Hugh Laurie, Jonathan Miller, David Mitchell, Emma Thompson and Sandi Toksvig.

Thus, the extraordinary achievements of Cambridge in the last half millennium make a few comments by Erasmus pale into insignificance.

INTRODUCTION

This book uses photographs to show Cambridge as it was in the past and as it is today. Yet it is not simply past and present that are contrasted. Cambridge is a market town into which a university was inserted, cuckoo-like, over 700 years ago. The contrast between university city and market town still persists.

For me, much of Cambridge University's architecture appeared at first sight to have remained unchanged for a century or more. However, after looking closely at historic photographs, I was surprised to see that significant changes had been made, particularly where town met gown. Gonville and Caius' huge gargoyles look as though they have brooded over Trinity Street for centuries, yet have done so only since 1870, as old photographs testify. Sometimes, of course, radical changes were made before the arrival of photography. An example is Sidney Sussex College's Gothic stone facade: hidden below this early nineteenth-century makeover is the original Elizabethan red brick.

Elsewhere, however, both ancient and more recent colleges have remained unchanged. A court in Peterhouse (founded 1284) remains as unaltered as one in Selwyn (founded 1882). In these cases the contrasts between past and present reside in the photographs themselves. The monochrome picture of Selwyn (see page 124) seems special, since today we are less accustomed to black-and-white photography; my recent colour photograph, though less striking, brings out the hues of the building set against those of grass and sky. Though unrecorded in old photographs, such visual effects may have figured in the architect's conception.

A first look at the 'Then' and 'Now' photographs of Churchill College (see pages 132–33), a twentieth-century foundation, may reveal no change, but looking closer one spots the usual 'Health and Safety' additions (protective balustrade and so on) that older colleges have kept at bay. With Murray Edwards, we can see the college under construction in the early 1960s (see page 134). If only, one feels, photography had been invented before King's College Chapel had been completed.

To see the Backs and King's College Chapel for the first time is a hugely satisfying experience – for this, after all, is one of the greatest views in the world. The awe-inspiring fifteenth-century chapel can compete with the Parthenon or the Taj Mahal as one of the most elegant buildings on Earth. There are many buildings in Cambridge that boast splendid features – the magisterial Wren Library, graceful Clare Bridge, the Roman facade of the Fitzwilliam Museum. And yet, contrasting with such grandeur, the experience of less imposing effects is something that gives Cambridge its special charm. These milder satisfactions need to be sought out. Sauntering into Trinity Hall, resting on a bench while appreciating the Queen Anne-revival architecture of Newnham,

or meandering through the informal gardens of Murray Edwards are quiet pleasures whose memory lingers.

As for the city itself, changes during the period when photography could record them have been surprisingly few compared with other British cities. True, buildings have been demolished to be replaced by college extensions – the transition sometimes witnessed by many onlookers, as in the 1904 photograph of a building's last moments before it made way for the new city library (see page 112). The post-war period saw the greatest changes to the city centre, such as the erection of the Lion Yard shopping centre in 1970, with its cumbersome concrete car park. More recently, much greater care has been taken to retain the facades of those buildings that already blend into the streetscape. Sayle's department store frontage remains, having been sensitively converted (in part) into the city's Magistrates' Court. The entrance through the former store into the Grand Arcade shopping mall was sufficiently well disguised for me to have to ask where it was. Few other shopping mall entrances can be as discreet as this.

Unlike its rival city, Oxford, Cambridge does not suffer from flocks of buses clogging up its city centre. This is partly because its smaller streets cannot accommodate traffic so easily. But it also seems to be the result of better planning. In Cambridge I didn't have to wait for the split second between one bus and the next to take the street photographs for this book. Setting up a photograph of a Cambridge street at the place where a forerunner had done so was a far pleasanter experience than in Oxford. This was welcome, since my favourite part of the city is its centre. Standing in Petty Cury early one summer morning outside a shop where, according to a photograph in my hand (see opposite), you could once buy a suit for £1.85, reminded me that Cambridge was not so dissimilar to the small market town, Newark-upon-Trent, in which I was brought up. The only things giving the game away were the grand pinnacles of King's College Chapel rising behind this modest scene.

Around the corner from Petty Cury is the Market Hill, where Cambridge started in Anglo-Saxon times. Now as then, it is the place to buy and sell. Here I took the photograph that is my personal favourite (see page 109). When the lady standing at the market stall left, I went to buy fruit and veg myself. Afterwards it occurred to me that this would probably not be possible at the centre of any other great university city. Perhaps it is being able to do things like this that makes Cambridge, as both market town and university city, so cherishably unique.

Vaughan Grylls, March 2011

HOBSON'S CONDUIT

Named after the man who
coined the well-known phrase

Until 1856 Hobson's Conduit was situated in the
Market Place, as seen here, which makes this
undated photograph amongst the oldest in this book.
The idea of supplying fresh water from outside the
town first came in 1574 from Andrew Perne, Master
of Peterhouse, and although nothing was done at the
time, Perne's proposal was later revived by James
Montagu, Master of Sidney Sussex College. Through
channels, which still run alongside Trumpington
Street, fresh water arrived at the Market Place in
1614. The channelling costs were shared by town and
gown, but the design and construction of this water
outlet was paid for by Thomas Hobson, landlord of the
George Inn and owner of livery stables in Cambridge
and London. Apart from having his name attached to
it, Hobson achieved greater immortality through what
was to become a well-known saying. Rather than
allowing his customer to choose a horse, which was
the accepted convention of the time, Hobson
presented the horse that had been in his stables the
longest. Those who objected were bluntly given
Hobson's choice: this horse or no horse.

Hobson's Conduit was exiled to the junction of Trumpington Street and Lensfield Road following a fire in the Market Place in 1856. By this time, the spread of piped fresh water into Cambridge had made the conduit less necessary. Visitors arriving from the south might not notice Hobson's Conduit as it is set back in a small garden. In any case, by the time they reach this road junction, the visitor's attention will probably be taken by the impressive facade of the Fitzwilliam Museum (see following page). Hobson's Conduit now sits on a plinth making it appear more of a sculpted monument. Although it has been restored, and water no longer flows from its recesses, its quirky design yet practical intent provides an apt memorial for its benefactor.

THE FITZWILLIAM MUSEUM

One of the world's finest museums

Left: The Fitzwilliam Museum owes its name to the 7th Viscount FitzWilliam who bequeathed £100,000 for a building – together with his collection of paintings, etchings, books and medieval illuminated manuscripts – to the University of Cambridge in 1815. The Fitzwilliam's architect was George Basevi, a pupil of Sir John Soane. Basevi had studied architecture in Italy and Greece and it is likely that his design was informed by the remains of a Roman Capitolium discovered at Brescia in 1820. Work on the Fitzwilliam started in 1837 and was due to be completed by 1848. However, in 1845 Basevi plunged to his death from scaffolding at Ely Cathedral. Charles Cockerell was brought in to redesign the entrance hall and in 1871–75 the museum was given another makeover by Edward Middleton Barry. Judging from the clothes of the passers-by, this photograph was taken during or soon after World War I. For a woman to wear black at this time usually signified the loss of a loved one.

Above: The firm of Smith & Brewer extended the Fitzwilliam in 1924 with the addition of the Marley Galleries, and again in 1931–36 with the Courtauld and Henderson Galleries. The architect David Roberts provided further extensions in 1966 and 1975. An interior rebuild was completed in 2004 by John Miller & Partners. In this photograph, the exterior has been cleaned and renovations continue. The Fitzwilliam boasts a collection of major European and Asian works, including the Macclesfield Psalter depicting scenes from early fourteenth-century England. Although it does not possess a large collection, in quality it owns one of the world's best. George Basevi, the Fitzwilliam's principal architect was not to be the only person to affect the museum with an inadvertent tumble. In 2006 a visitor from the nearby village of Fowlmere tripped on a loose shoelace, fell down the stairs, and hit three irreplaceable Qing Dynasty seventeenth-century Chinese vases, smashing them into small shards. Amazingly, they have since been restored and now sit in protective cases.

OLD ADDENBROOKE'S HOSPITAL / JUDGE BUSINESS SCHOOL

Two leading research and teaching institutes

Left: Addenbrooke's Hospital was opened in 1766 on land purchased in 1728 on Trumpington Street. The land was bequeathed by John Addenbrooke (1680–1719) for the establishment of a hospital for the poor. Addenbrooke was a medical doctor and a Fellow of St Catharine's College, to whom he left his medical library. Over the next century Addenbrooke's Hospital was expanded to meet demands, to the extent that it became necessary to redesign it substantially. The building we see here was completed in 1863 by the architect Matthew Digby Wyatt. The hospital is shown in 1911 celebrating the coronation of King George V.

Below: In 1994 the Old Addenbrooke's Hospital site, as it became known when the new hospital opened on Hills Road, was converted into the Judge Institute of Management Studies. Now known as the Judge Business School, it is part of the Faculty of Business & Management at the University of Cambridge. In 1954 the architectural historian Nicholas Pevsner had dismissed Wyatt's design as 'a depressing example of its date, with many rather dry, thin motifs, Italian as well as Tudor, assembled without any tension or accentuation.' Whatever one's personal views on its 1994 post-modernist makeover by the architect John Outram, the full effects of which can be seen inside the building, its new top floor does appear to address Pevsner's comments with its more decisive silhouette. The new Addenbrooke's Hospital and the Judge Business School are regarded in their fields as being amongst the leading teaching and research institutions in the world.

TRUMPINGTON STREET, LOOKING TOWARDS THE FITZWILLIAM MUSEUM

Now dominated by the spire of the United Reform Church

Left: This photograph was taken in 1862. Trumpington Street was then cobbled, as were most city streets in England. The roadside channels were first installed in 1788 to take fresh water from springs to the south of Cambridge, via the Cambridge New River to Hobson's Conduit on Market Hill. By the time of this photo, however, the role of Hobson's Conduit had been replaced by piped water. The channels replaced one first laid in 1610 down the middle of the road. To the left is the fourteenth-century facade of Pembroke College, followed by the college's iconic chapel (1663–65) with its projecting pediment and cupola. This was architect Christopher Wren's first completed work and it marks the introduction of Renaissance architecture into the city. In the distance can be seen the apex of the Fitzwilliam Museum's pediment.

Above: The main change is to the right with the introduction of the Emmanuel Congregational (now United Reformed) Church. The church was designed by James Cubitt and completed in 1875. Cubitt's cumbersome spire asserts itself on the Cambridge skyline as well as on Trumpington Street. Although an inelegant church, it does contain some interesting Victorian glass representations of prominent Cambridge-educated Protestants, including Henry Barrow and John Greenwood – both hanged at Tyburn in 1593 – as well as flattering portraits of Oliver Cromwell and John Milton.

FIRST COURT, PETERHOUSE

The oldest college in Cambridge

Peterhouse (never Peterhouse College) is the oldest college in Cambridge. It was founded by Hugh de Balsham, Bishop of Ely, in 1284. Peterhouse's entrance, First Court, which opens onto Trumpington Street, is seen here sometime in the 1950s. The classical entrance gate dates from the eighteenth century, as does the Burrough's Building on the left. On the other side of Trumpington Street can be seen Wren's chapel for Pembroke College and to the right Pembroke's residential buildings designed by Alfred Waterhouse and built in 1871–72.

Besides the increase in the number and variety of bicycles, the lengthier plaque of rules and the permanent closure of the eighteenth-century entrance gate (entrance to the college is now via the Porter's Lodge behind the photographer), First Court has changed very little in half a century. Perhaps this is unsurprising, as traditionally Peterhouse is regarded as the most conservative in attitude of the Cambridge colleges. Alfred Waterhouse's abundant use of red brick across the street becomes apparent in this colour photograph.

OLD COURT, PETERHOUSE

Incorporating architectural styles from the thirteenth to the nineteenth century

Above: Recorded here in the 1950s by the eminent architectural photographer Eric de Maré, the most striking part of Old Court is the far side with its chapel built in 1628–34. This presents a truly transitional design by blending the architecture of the medieval period with that of the Renaissance. The colonnades on either side, which lead onto First Court, do the same. The building to the left appears to date from the eighteenth century. However, this facade, designed by Sir James Burrough, Master of Caius, and built in 1754, in fact covers thirteenth- to fifteenth-century structures. The building on the right houses the dining hall, dating from the thirteenth century, although it was extensively rebuilt, albeit in a medieval style, by George Gilbert Scott, the younger, in 1870. Its interior is decorated by William Morris.

Right: Unusually, Old Court appears to have had no renovation to its stonework in over half a century. That is not to say that it has been aesthetically overlooked. Its colourful window box displays and the care and attention lavished on its courtyard lawn, cobbling and flagstones show the college in anticipation of the start of a new academic year. The Victorian-style lamp standards have probably been introduced as a health and safety requirement, blending, as is often the case nowadays, instant history with the needs of the modern world. Famous alumni of Peterhouse include the designer of the forerunner of the modern computer, Charles Babbage; the designer of the forerunner of the modern jet engine, Frank Whittle; the Hollywood film star James Mason; the theatre and film directors Richard Eyre and Sam Mendes; the Gold Medal Pentathlon champion Steph Cook; and the comedian and writer David Mitchell.

TRUMPINGTON STREET AND LITTLE ST MARY'S LANE

Site of the old Half Moon Inn

Left: This photograph was taken in 1875 and shows the old Half Moon Inn at the corner of Little St Mary's Lane and Trumpington Street. This was one of many inns built to provide bed and board for stagecoach travellers between London, Cambridge, East Anglia and the North. Coaches and stabling would be provided at the rear, accessed through the arch at the side. With the arrival of the railways, many inns were closed or became solely public houses.

Right: It is often said that if one is looking for a pub in an unfamiliar town, first identify the church spire and you will then find a pub opposite or nearby. In this unusual case, one has had to make way for the other. The Half Moon Inn was demolished and James Cubitt's Emmanuel Congregational (now United Reformed) Church was built on its site in 1875. The adjacent buildings have remained intact, except for the removal of a dormer and a first-floor pediment on one of the houses. In the distance is the Pitt Building – once the headquarters of Cambridge University Press, it is now a conference and meetings centre owned and operated by CUP.

THE STREET FRONTAGE
OF PEMBROKE COLLEGE

Blending medieval, Renaissance and Victorian styles of architecture

Left: The renowned architectural photographer A.F. Kersting took this photograph using his signature long exposure (see the bicyclist) in the late 1940s/early 1950s. Pembroke can trace its foundation to 1347, making it the third oldest college in Cambridge. Three of Pembroke's architectural styles span the right-hand side of Trumpington Street in this photo. In the distance are the oldest buildings in the college, dating to the latter half of the fourteenth century. Just behind the car on the right is the main entrance to the college, the oldest gatehouse in Cambridge. These buildings, which form part of Old Court, were refaced in 1712–17 in pale ashlar stone. The cupola belongs to Christopher Wren's splendid Pembroke College Chapel built in 1663–65, the first purely Renaissance building to be constructed in Cambridge and the architect's first ecclesiastical commission. Far right are Alfred Waterhouse's 'Red Buildings', constructed in 1871–72. In the first part of the twentieth century, Waterhouse's work fell out of fashion, resulting in some architectural tinkering, yet not improvement, in 1925 and 1949.

Above: Little has changed to the scene in over sixty years, other than the ubiquitous double yellow lines and the church railings of Little St Mary's Church (left) that now attract posters. An open channel that once carried fresh water to Hobson's Conduit in Market Hill can be seen running between road and pavement. This is called the Pot, after 'Pothouse' (an old nickname for Peterhouse). Its sister channel opposite, called the Pem for obvious reasons, is just out of sight owing to the curvature of the road. The street frontage of Pembroke College provides a narrative of three of the principal styles in the history of English architecture – medieval, Renaissance and Victorian. It would be difficult to find a more succinct triptych in the whole country. Famous alumni of the college include politicians William Pitt the Younger and R.A. Butler; poets Thomas Gray and Ted Hughes; and comedians Peter Cook and Tim Brook-Taylor.

THE PITT BUILDING

Its late-Gothic appearance earned it the nickname
of the 'Freshman's Church'

The Pitt Building was built between 1831 and 1833 for
the world's oldest publisher, the Cambridge
University Press. CUP was founded by letters patent
from Henry VIII in 1534. Its architect was Edward
Blore and the money to build it came from surplus
subscriptions collected for a memorial to William Pitt
the Younger, Prime Minister during the Napoleonic
Wars and former student of Pembroke College.
Undergraduates called it the 'Freshman's Church'
because of its late-Gothic style of architecture. Its
ecclesiastical appearance made it the building of
choice for the practical joke of directing new students
there for Sabbath worship. The two-letter, four-digit
registration numbers of the cars give this photograph
a pre-1932 date.

As in most cases with stone buildings in Cambridge, soot has been cleaned from the facings. However, the biggest change is to the first- and second-floor windows – which were widened in 1934–37 by Murray Easton. His modernisation meant that the Pitt Building was less likely to be mistaken for a church. Due to its altered appearance and the gradual disappearance of piety over the years, the 'Freshman's Church' title has become an anachronism. Although most of Cambridge University Press's activities now take place in a large modern complex near the main railway station, the publishers still retain the Pitt Building for some of their work.

25

TRUMPINGTON STREET
AND ST BOTOLPH'S CHURCH

The nave of this Grade I listed church dates back to 1350

Left: This marvellous photograph, looking north towards King's Parade and taken in 1862, shows St Botolph's Church on the right. In the centre distance is the east end of King's College Chapel. To the left is St Catharine's College, while to the right, just beyond St Botolph's, is Corpus Christi College. The boy leaning against the railings may have taken up his pose for the photographer's farthing, a practice commonly employed to give the main building in the photograph scale, as well as making the scene more picturesque. The only unusual feature is the couple on the left. Their blurred image reminds us that the Victorian camera needed a long exposure. Their image also begs two questions – whether the photographer asked the couple to pause briefly for the photograph (if so they must have refused) and why a Victorian gentleman is escorting a lady from the inside of the pavement.

Above: To the right the buildings are unchanged. While St Botolph's Church dates back to the fourteenth and fifteenth century its predecessors stood here long before. Its site was probably chosen because this is where a city gate once stood and Botolph was a patron saint of travellers. To the left the group of buildings has either been demolished or so extensively remodelled as to appear completely different. These changes would have been under the auspices of St Catharine's College, which owns this land and property. Also to the left, what appears to be a Cambridge tradition of ignoring escorting etiquette continues apace.

ST CATHARINE'S COLLEGE

Founded on St Catharine's Day in 1473

St Catharine's College was founded by Robert Woodlark, Provost of King's College, on St Catharine's Day, 25 November 1473. Originally called Catharine Hall, it took the title of St Catharine's College in 1860. The Main Court, known sometimes as the Principal Court, was built in the late seventeenth century by the master mason Robert Grumbold, although for this building he mainly used brick. A Mr Elder from London advised the college on its design. Throughout its first century Main Court was hidden behind houses fronting Trumpington Street. Their demolition in the eighteenth century allowed its three sides to be seen clearly by passers-by. Here Main Court is seen in 1925.

The twentieth-century architect Sir Hugh Casson described Main Court as presenting 'a mild, modest and rosy face' demonstrated here in the subdued brickwork, the stonework detailing and the dormers, with their alternating triangular and almost semi-circular pediments. However, alternating pediments were not used for the chapel, dating from 1694 and standing to the immediate right in this photograph. Alumni of St Catharine's include founder of Cambridge's hospital, John Addenbrooke, author Malcolm Lowry, theatre director Sir Peter Hall, actor Sir Ian McKellan and broadcaster Jeremy Paxman.

SILVER STREET

One of the best-preserved examples of medieval brickwork in Cambridge

This fifteenth-century brick wall on Silver Street, photographed here in the 1950s, forms the southern boundary of Queens' College. Although understandably worn and in need of repointing, the brickwork appears to have weathered rather better than the stonework in the intervening half millennium. Nevertheless, even in the 1950s, this rear wall of Queens' College's Old Court was perhaps the best-preserved medieval brick wall fronting a Cambridge street. Its architect is thought to have been Reginald Ely, the King's mason, who also designed King's College, Eton, and King's College, Cambridge. Similar architectural cues are used in all three. In this handsomely framed and lit photograph, a student attired in collar and tie provides the scale this image needs.

Apart from the change from monochrome to colour, and the comparative informality of the figure in the foreground (Ms J.E. Gong of South Korea), little seems to have changed in the intervening half century. However, a closer inspection reveals very extensive refurbishment. The stonework has been replaced, or at least renovated, and the Victorian drainpipe has been replaced with a modern medieval version. The most interesting change is to the brickwork, which has been cleaned and repointed, revealing the architect's subtle patterning on the lower reaches.

CLOISTER COURT, QUEENS' COLLEGE

Margaret of Anjou and Elizabeth Woodville
are the patrons who gave the college its name

Left: Queens' College, founded in 1448 by a local clergyman, Andrew Dockett, has the apostrophe after the 's' because its name refers to more than one patron: Margaret of Anjou, wife of Henry VI, followed by Elizabeth Woodville, wife of Edward IV. The husband of the second deposed the husband of the first in the Wars of the Roses. While each of the wings of Cloister Court, photographed here in the 1950s by Eric de Maré, was built in a different century the presence of a covered cloister remains. The brick building to the left dates from around 1460 to 1495. Built perhaps to house distinguished guests, it now contains the President's Lodge. The President's Gallery, the half-timbered building to the right, is late sixteenth century and was built in the style of a Tudor country house to contain the then-fashionable long gallery. The central oriel window supported by wooden pillars succeeds in this building as a focal point as well as lending distinct charm.

Below: Other than the planting, nothing has substantially changed to this scene. The time of day, deliberately chosen by the 'Then' photographer, reveals the modelling and texture of the covered cloister. In the 'Now' image the emphasis changes to the play of colours between the buildings of Cloister Court, all held together by the immaculate greensward. Alumni include a father of the Renaissance, Erasmus of Rotterdam (although he was at Queens' College from 1511 to 1514, officially he was only staying there, which didn't stop him being consistently rude about it, especially the quality of its wine and beer); bishop and martyr John Fisher; composer Charles Villiers Stanford; Foreign Minister of Israel, Abba Eban; the first British man in space, Michael Foale; and comedian and author Stephen Fry.

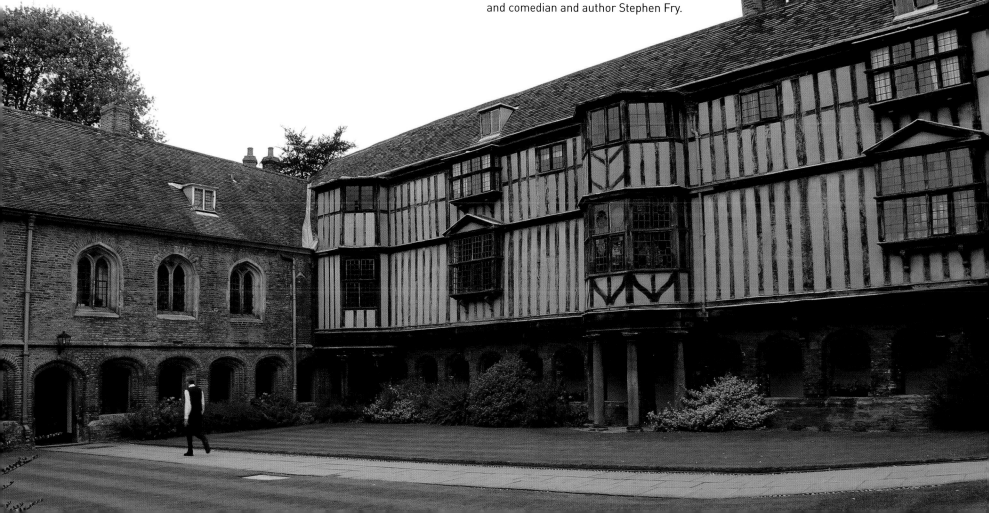

THE MATHEMATICAL BRIDGE, QUEENS' COLLEGE

This wooden bridge has been rebuilt twice since it first crossed the Cam in 1750

Left: Although it is known as the Mathematical Bridge, its correct name, according to Queens' College, is simply the Wooden Bridge. It was originally constructed in 1749–50 by James Essex from a design by Queens' undergraduate William Etheridge. The bridge was rebuilt in 1867 and again in 1902. While William Etheridge was a student he visited China, which may help explain the bridge's almost oriental character. The riverside of the mid-fifteenth century section of Queens' Cloister Court is shown to good effect in this 1950s photograph.

Above: Because the Wooden Bridge has been rebuilt every century, it would be fair to think that a completely new version is overdue. However, a construction like this is now more likely be replaced in parts and repaired as required rather than entirely rebuilt. While this relatively new 'conservation' approach has been applied to all of Cambridge's colleges, a century or more ago it would have been considered strange. The way the Cam is used has also changed with the centuries. Today's punting tourists pay to enter a slower, gentler age. It may surprise visitors to know that before the riverside colleges introduced their impressive buildings and beautiful grounds, the dreamy river on which they float was flanked by noisy, bustling wharves, a key element in the commercial growth of early medieval Cambridge.

OLD COURT, CORPUS CHRISTI COLLEGE

The oldest complete court in Cambridge

Above: Old Court, shown here in the 1950s, was built between 1352 and 1377. As its name suggests, it is the oldest complete court in Cambridge. Behind is the Saxon tower of St Bene't's, the oldest building in Cambridge, which dates back to the eleventh century. Thanks to its proximity, and because until around 1500 the college used the church as its chapel, Corpus Christi was known colloquially as Bene't College. Corpus Christi was founded in 1352 by a Cambridge town guild dedicated to the Body of Christ (Corpus Christi) and the Blessed Virgin Mary and is the only college in Oxford or Cambridge founded by town rather than gown. It owes its establishment to the Black Death of 1349, which killed at least one-third of Europe's population. After the plague, what remained of the guild's assets were supplemented by those members who had survived and the sum was used to establish the college, whose avowed purpose was to provide religious succour to the few remaining members, to pray for the souls of those departed, and to teach students – when they found the time.

Right: Old Court was originally built with stone rubble and faced in Barnack limestone, but this was plastered over in the early twentieth century. The stone buttresses were added in the fifteenth and sixteenth century. The garret windows and chimneys are sixteenth century additions. To the left of the sundial a missing suspended lamp has been replaced, which is to be expected of Corpus Christi; one of the richest Cambridge colleges with the smallest undergraduate student intake. Distinguished alumni of Corpus Christi include playwright Christopher Marlowe; novelist Christopher Isherwood; neurobiologist Professor Colin Blakemore; journalists Simon Heffer, Tom Utley and Madeleine Bunting; actor Hugh Bonneville; and historian and peace campaigner E.P. Thompson.

THE EAGLE, BENE'T STREET

Where the double-helix model of DNA was first announced

Left: The Eagle dates from 1667 and was known originally as the Eagle and Child. It is owned by Corpus Christi College, which is beyond St Bene't's Church, opposite the pub. The galleried courtyard is photographed here in the 1940s and looks as shabby as most pubs did before they transformed themselves, in relatively recent times, into food and drink venues attractive to women as well as men. It is the most famous pub in Cambridge and there must be few university members who have not visited it during its long history.

Above: Since the 1940s more has happened to the Eagle than suggested by this makeover, including here the obligatory hanging flower baskets and the continental-style outdoor seating. During World War II, the Eagle became popular with aircrew and the signatures and graffiti of those who came back from operations and those who didn't can be seen on the walls and ceilings of the 'RAF' bar. The most celebrated event at the Eagle took place at lunchtime on 23 February 1953 when two Cambridge scientists, Francis Crick and James Watson, burst in announcing to the assembled drinkers that they had just 'discovered the secret of life'. That may have driven God-fearing and God-less clientele alike to order another. A blue plaque outside the Eagle commemorates the informal manner in which the discovery that DNA carries genetic information was announced. The 'baths' sign, which has only been recently uncovered, is likely to have been an advertisement aimed at tired and dusty coaching travellers before the railway age, when such an amenity was a tempting attraction.

THE BULL HOTEL,
KING'S PARADE

This former hotel and military headquarters is now a part of St Catharine's College

Left: Grand Victorian hotels such as the Bull were developed with the arrival of the railways. This building, owned by St Catharine's College, dates from 1828 and was leased to a Mr Crisford. In 1843 it was opened as the Bull Hotel. The Bull prided itself on providing 'warm, cold and shower-baths adjoining the bed-chambers' to the 'Nobility, Gentry and Public' and it was later claimed that it was 'much frequented by royalty, Australians and Americans'. Mr Crisford and his successors had a clear idea into which social category their clientele should be placed. Nevertheless, the Americans must have appreciated the Bull for during World War II, after requisition by the British military from St Catharine's, the hotel was accepted as a US military headquarters, as seen here in 1944.

Above: After the war, the link with America continued through the establishment of Bull College, which provided a Cambridge degree programme for American GIs throughout 1945 and 1946 as part of the US Army's 'Training Within Civilian Agencies' programme. Yet like many buildings requisitioned in the war, the Bull never returned to its former use and it is now integrated into St Catharine's College. To the right of the former entrance passage to the Bull's yard is the King's Parade frontage of King's Lane Courts designed in 1965–68 by Fello Atkinson of James Cubitt and Partners. It was built on the site of the Bull's yard with a bequest from John Maynard Keynes. It is shared by King's College and St Catharine's College and houses a dining hall and underground car park for the former and a concert hall (Keynes Hall) for the latter. The gloomy passage leading to these developments is somewhat grandly designated King's Lane.

VICTORIAN PILLAR-BOX, KING'S PARADE

An original British icon

This elegant Victorian pillar-box, photographed not long after World War II, stands next to the gatehouse of King's College on King's Parade. This is a genuine Penfold Type PB 8/1 box, named after its designer, the architect John Wornham Penfold. His was the first pillar box to be manufactured in the new standard colour of red in 1874 and it can still be seen throughout the former British Empire, if infrequently in Britain itself.

Pillar-box red can be seen in its full resplendence here. Replicas of the Penfold pillar-box have since become fashionable, providing instant history wherever it is felt to be required. There is even a replica Penfold erected in the centre of Singapore with the sole purpose of accepting Christmas cards. Here, outside King's College, the Penfold's stone background has been cleaned and there are some refreshingly blunt signs.

FRONT COURT AND GATEHOUSE, KING'S COLLEGE

William Wilkins' finest Gothic Revival achievement

Left: The first impression given by this 1940s photograph of the vast Front Court of King's College is one of medieval grand scale. In a sense this is true, except that these buildings date from 1824–28. They are the work of the celebrated architect William Wilkins and here his style is flamboyant Gothic Revival, although he was equally at home with the restrained classical, as demonstrated by the National Gallery and University College London. Wilkins' gatehouse and screen, which separates Front Court from King's Parade, is perhaps his finest Gothic Revival achievement. King's College was founded in 1441 by Henry VI with relatively modest intentions, but by 1445 he decided that this was where the pupils of his recently established school at Eton should be admitted exclusively, an arrangement which continued rather curiously for over 400 years.

Right: In this wider-angled view, Wilkins' range of buildings on the south side can also be seen. To the right is part of the College Hall, with one of its two three-tiered timber lanterns just in view. These were rebuilt in 1950–51 by W.F. Haslop of the local builders Rattee and Kett. In the centre of Front Court stands a statue of its founder Henry VI. Distinguished alumni of King's include the first Prime Minister Robert Walpole; art critic Roger Fry; poet Rupert Brooke; philosopher George Santayana; economist John Maynard Keynes; code-breaker and computer scientist Alan Turing; journalist Johann Hari; comedian David Baddiel; and novelists E.M. Forster, J.G. Ballard, Salman Rushdie and Zadie Smith.

KING'S COLLEGE CHAPEL FROM THE BACKS

This peaceful scene was once the bustling centre of medieval Cambridge

This is one of the most timeless images of England. To the left in this 1950s photograph is the magnificent Perpendicular Gothic west front of King's College Chapel (1446–1515); to the right the classical Fellows' or Gibbs Building by James Gibbs (1724–32). Immediately in front of these iconic buildings is the immaculate Back Lawn, followed by the Cam, which is hardly visible here. In the immediate foreground is the artfully informal meadow, Scholars' Piece. Here the English picturesque becomes real. King's College Chapel was a late arrival as Gothic architecture goes. During the time it was being built some of the great Renaissance buildings of continental Europe, especially in Italy, were being constructed. Yet the beautiful symmetry and proportions of this magnificent building hint at a knowledge of this rebirth of classicism. In 1448 Henry VI himself determined his chapel's specifications and, as a king with a continental realm of his own, it is quite possible that he would have been aware of architectural developments in Europe.

In this contemporary photograph, part of the sunlit south wing of Clare College (1640–42) can be seen on the left. Thus, in one sweep we can view architecture from the fifteenth to the eighteenth centuries. Yet it is to King's College and specifically to the play between two of its buildings, one Gothic the other Classical, set in a country landscape, that we are drawn. It may be difficult to imagine but this was once the bustling centre of medieval Cambridge. Streets, houses, shops,

wharves, a church (St John Zachary) and even a recently completed college (God's House, the forerunner of Christ's College) were all ruthlessly destroyed to make way for Henry VI's new college, its extensive grounds and what has since become one of the most celebrated scenes in England.

KING'S PARADE, LOOKING NORTH

Including St Catharine's College, King's College and Senate House

Left: This is how King's Parade appeared in 1911. From left to right, we see a small business, Marshall & Kiddy; the Bull Hotel; a bay-windowed part of King's College; the screen and gatehouse of King's College; the south pediment and wings of the Senate House; and, peeping out on the horizon, the tower of St John's College Chapel. When this photograph was taken, this substantial building by Sir George Gilbert Scott was only forty-two years old. For many years Scott's tower was considered a bulky and lofty intrusion (see page 73). To the right are houses of various dates with Victorian crenulated bay windows, giving way to an oriel window further down. The roadway provides a snapshot of the transition from a horse-powered to a motorised world at a time when the British Empire had reached its height.

Above: The small business on the left has disappeared or been heavily remodelled by St Catharine's College, its current owners. The Bull Hotel, also owned by St Catharine's, no longer exists. The building, minus its entrance canopy, remains intact and is now an integral part of the college. Beyond is the King's Parade frontage of King's Lane Courts, designed by Fello Atkinson of James Cubitt and Partners in 1965-68. Sophisticated motorised vehicles for the disabled would have seemed astonishing, if not inconceivable, when the 'Then' photograph was taken.

KING'S PARADE WITH UNDERGRADUATES

Encompassing Senate House, Gonville and Caius College,
and the Church of St Mary the Great

Left: To many, this spot is considered to be the centre of Cambridge University. Far left is James Gibbs' 1722–30 Baroque-inspired Senate House; to its immediate right is Alfred Waterhouse's 1868–70 French Renaissance-style addition to Gonville and Caius College. Ahead, King's Parade turns into Trinity Street, from where you can reach Gonville and Caius, Trinity, Trinity Hall and St John's colleges. On the far right, just peeping into frame, is the church of St Mary the Great, often called the University Church, not least because until 1730 it acted as the Senate House. There has been a church on this site since at least 1205, although this building dates to 1478–1519. Here a group of undergraduates saunter along a wet King's Parade in late 1939, soon after the outbreak of World War II. This was the period of 'The Phoney War', an eerie time before the storm broke and nearly every young man rushed to the colours or was called up if he didn't.

Below: In the late eighteenth and early nineteenth centuries, many old merchant houses and even the Provost's Lodge of King's College were demolished here to provide a broad and uncluttered street. The intention was to provide pedestrians with an undisturbed view of the new Senate House and St Mary the Great. In more recent times, pedestrianisation has hit Cambridge in full force. This scene includes all of the trappings of a modern pedestrianised area: bollards imitating those that were once used for tying horses to, old-fashioned cobbles, concrete benches, empty concrete planters, Victorian-style waste bins and signs reminding cyclists which side of the road to pedal on. This photograph was taken one early morning following a May Ball, where, traditionally, final-year Cambridge undergraduates let their hair down for the last time before leaving university for the big wide world.

VIEW FROM THE TOWER OF ST MARY THE GREAT CHURCH

Encompassing some of Cambridge University's most important buildings

Above: There are few old photographs of this view from the tower of St Mary the Great, which is not surprising. Carrying a heavy plate camera up 123 steps of a medieval turret staircase would not have been for the faint-hearted. This badly damaged photograph was taken in 1892. It shows King's College Old Court, the original gatehouse and buildings, sold to the university in 1829 for use as administrative offices. It dates to 1441 but stood unfinished until 1864–67 when George Gilbert Scott undertook work on the buildings, which were finally completed by J.L. Pearson in 1890. Behind is Clare College's Old Court dating to 1669. The prominent roof to the right is C.R. Cockerell's Cambridge University Library (1837–42).

Right: This all-encompassing view focuses on the ceremonial and administrative centre of Cambridge University. Stephen Wright's 1754–58 neo-Palladian frontage, to the east range of Cobble Court, dominates. Wright's New Library replaced a medieval entrance. Little of the original medieval structure remains behind this splendid facade. In the right foreground is James Gibbs' 1722–30 Senate House. Here university ceremonies are held, culminating in the Summer General Admissions where senior be-robed university officials process to the Senate House, escorting those about to receive honorary degrees. Behind Senate House is Cockerell's building, now the library of Caius College. Far left is King's College Chapel. On the horizon is the latest University Library (1931–34) by Giles Gilbert Scott. Its massive central tower commands the Cambridge skyline, even from the M11, some miles away. It would be difficult to find a more impressive group of university administrative buildings anywhere else.

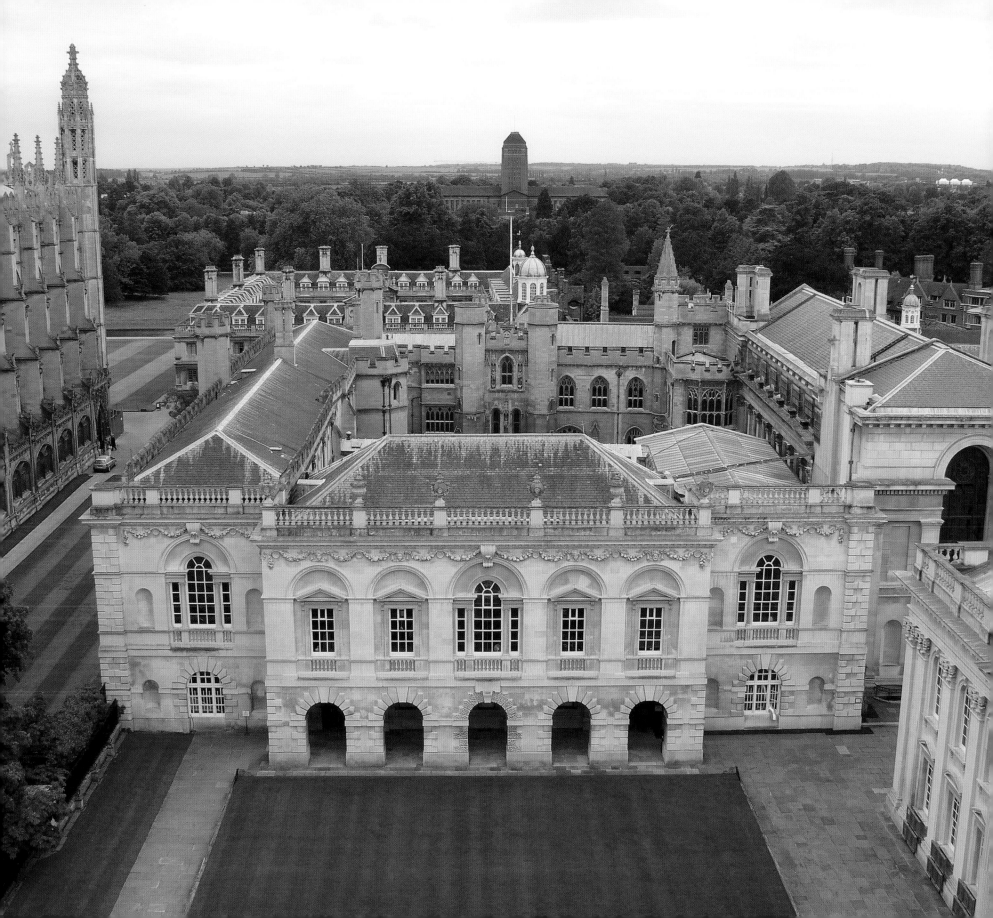

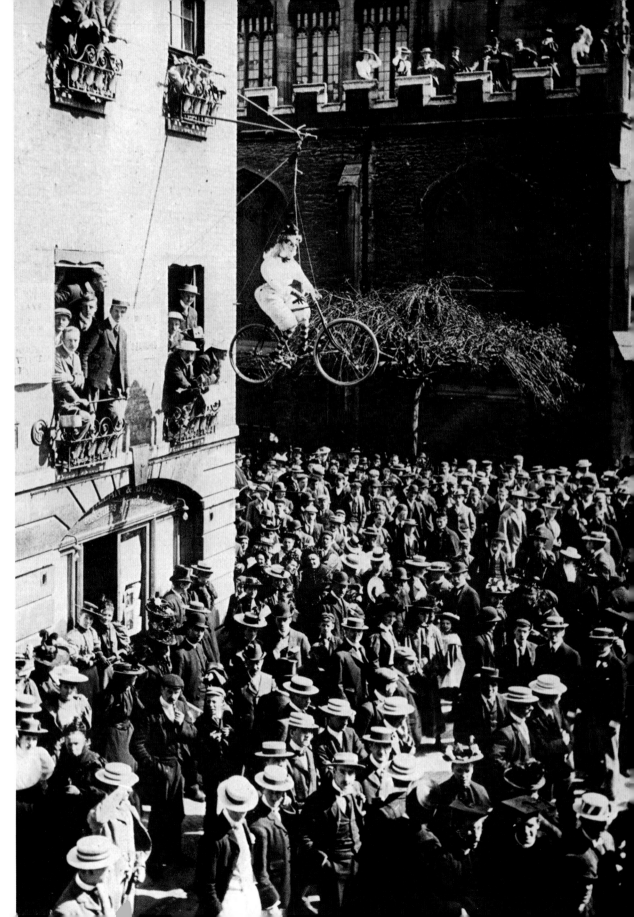

THE CORNER OF KING'S PARADE AND ST MARY'S STREET

The site of demonstrations against proposals to grant women degrees in 1897

At the time this photograph was being taken in 1897, Cambridge University was counting the votes in the Senate House on whether to grant degrees to women. Cambridge MAs had the right to vote and special trains were organised to bring to the city those who wished to take part, which helps explain why most of the people in this photograph are men. Suspended on a bicycle from the window of Macmillan & Bowes bookshop, is a female mannequin clad in bloomers. Here the onlookers include those on the roof of the north aisle of the Church of St Mary the Great (also known as the University Church), which, as the precursor of the Senate House, was once the centre of the university's ceremony and administration. The outcome of the voting was 1713 against, 662 in favour. In 1921 women were allowed degrees in title only but not in substance. It was not until 1948 that a female undergraduate could receive a degree fully equivalent to that of a man.

The building from which the mannequin in bloomers once projected still houses a bookshop, although now it is the Cambridge University Press. The church, owned by Trinity College and commonly called Great St Mary's, has few university functions left. Besides University Sermons, which are still held here, the church expects undergraduates to live within three miles radius during term time; university staff within twenty. Galleries were added to the interior in 1735 to accommodate its overflowing congregation. The church also houses the university's organ and clock. The chimes for the latter, known as the Cambridge Chimes, were copied for the Houses of Parliament clock tower, Big Ben. Great St Mary's bell-ringers claim to be the oldest society of their kind in Britain. The church is built in the late Perpendicular Gothic style and most of what is seen today can be dated to 1478–1608, with various alterations and facelifts since. St Mary the Great's distinctive silhouette, established by its four corner turrets, was the work of master mason Robert Grumbold in 1608.

GONVILLE AND CAIUS COLLEGE AT TRINITY AND ST MARY'S STREET

Caius is pronounced 'Keys', after its re-founder John Keys

Left: Taken in the early 1950s, this attractive image by the architectural photographer A.F. Kersting shows this busy road junction at a time of post-war rationing when one cycled for economy rather than ecology. To the right a parson heads out of frame in the direction of Great St Mary's. On the other side, overlooking Trinity Street, and appearing overlarge, given the street's width, is a stretch of Gonville and Caius College.

Above: The sun lights up Gonville and Caius' confident stretch of French Renaissance-style architecture. This is a street-side part of Tree Court, a huge development by Alfred Waterhouse built for the college in 1868–70. The college is usually known simply as Caius, pronounced Keys, which is only understandable when one knows its re-founder was a philosopher and physician John Keys, who

had Latinised his name, probably because he had taught for many years in Padua. In 1557–58, having returned from Italy, he re-founded an impoverished Gonville Hall, first established by a Norfolk clergyman of that name in 1348 and which Caius had left as a Fellow in 1539. In 1559, John Caius himself became Master. Caius has a long-standing tradition in medical education and, apart from Trinity College Cambridge, has more Nobel laureates than any other Oxford or Cambridge college. Its alumni have gone on to distinguish themselves in many areas of endeavour, including architect William Wilkins; inventor of the Venn diagram, John Venn; Olympic athlete Harold Abrahams, discoverer of the circulation of the blood, William Harvey; discoverer of the neutron, Sir James Chadwick; joint discoverer of penicillin, Sir Howard Florey; physicist Stephen Hawking; joint discoverer of DNA, Sir Francis Crick; broadcaster Sir David Frost; and comedian Jimmy Carr.

TRINITY STREET AND ST MICHAEL'S CHURCH

The main thoroughfare from the city centre to some of the grandest colleges in Cambridge

In this photograph from 1868 Trinity Street appears narrow and cobbled. It is difficult to believe that this is the main thoroughfare from the city centre to some of the grandest colleges in Cambridge: Trinity, St John's, and Gonville and Caius, whose entrance is opposite the shabby looking church on the right. The church is St Michael's and it dates from the early fourteenth century. Its founder was Hervey de Stanton, who also founded Michaelhouse, a former Cambridge college, which was incorporated into Trinity College by Henry VIII. St Michael's once served as both a parish church and the chapel of Michaelhouse. Most of the other buildings in Trinity Street date to the seventeenth and eighteenth century. Before Trinity College was founded in 1546, this was known as the High Street. This photograph was probably taken for posterity, as the left side of the street was about to be demolished to make way for Alfred Waterhouse's Tree Court commissioned by Gonville and Caius College.

Alfred Waterhouse's giant gargoyles can be seen protruding from his large Tree Court development for Gonville and Caius, built in 1868–70. They look slightly out of scale and can cause a crick in the neck, even when viewed from the opposite pavement of this narrow street. St Michael's Church, now in better repair, contains a pleasant café where one can sit and admire from inside its large decorated window, seen here from the street. There is also a good set of medieval stalls, a sedilia (a group of stone seats) and an ogee-shaped doorway to attract one's attention. St Michael's Court, just beyond St Michael's Church, was built for Gonville and Caius by Sir Aston Webb in 1901–03. The statue on the corner is of physician and former Caius student William Harvey (1578–1657). In keeping with the appearance of many of England's medieval towns, Trinity Street has been pedestrianised and its old buildings smartened up by higher-end high-street chains. Of particular note is the black-and-white, timber-framed and gabled No. 14 (on the right-hand side of the street), which dates to the beginning of the seventeenth century. No. 20 is Heffers, Cambridge's principal bookshop, now owned by Blackwell's of Oxford.

TRINITY LANE

Including Caius and Trinity colleges

The impressive chimneys of Trinity Lane belong to the south range of Trinity College's Great Court, built between 1597 and 1615 under the auspices of Thomas Neville who was appointed Master in 1593 by Elizabeth I. To the left is Gonville and Caius College, with part of the north east corner of Alfred Waterhouse's Tree Court (1868–70). This strikingly lit photograph was taken by Eric de Maré in the 1950s.

In the intervening sixty years, the stonework of Neville's south range has been cleaned and the street lamps replaced by ones appearing more ancient. Double-yellow lines have appeared, as they have in most urban, picturesque and narrow lanes where one is still allowed to drive a car. So ubiquitous are they, we only notice them in photographs. The turrets of Queen's Gate, the southern gatehouse of Trinity College, can be seen at the end of the lane.

TRINITY HALL

Trinity's distinguished alumni includes Samuel Pepys, J.B. Priestley and Stephen Hawking

Left: Known to most as Trinity Hall – the college's formal name is 'the College of Scholars of the Holy Trinity of Norwich' – to many students it is known simply as 'Tit Hall'. Trinity Hall was founded by William Bateman, Bishop of Norwich, in 1350 as a college for the training of clergy and lawyers. Principal Court, in this 1940s photograph, dates from the late fourteenth century, although what we see here dates from 1741–45 when sash windows were inserted and the whole was sheathed in six-inch-thick ashlar by Sir James Burrough and James Essex the elder.

Right: Nikolaus Pevsner described this view as 'comfortable and a little phlegmatic'. Henry James was more positive. He wrote, 'If I were called upon to mention the prettiest corner of the world, I should draw a thoughtful sigh and point the way to the gardens of Trinity Hall.' Famous alumni of Trinity Hall include diarist Samuel Pepys; novelist J.B. Priestley; spy Donald Maclean; media theorist Marshall McLuhan; physicist Stephen Hawking; theatre and film director Nicholas Hytner; rower and Olympic Gold medallist Tom James; actress Rachel Weisz; and political commentator and journalist Andrew Marr.

CLARE COLLEGE

One of the most celebrated architectural views in Cambridge

This photograph from the early 1970s shows the Old Court at Clare College, one of the best architectural compositions in Cambridge University. It owes its confident uniformity to seventy-seven years of continuous building, from 1638 to 1715. Seen here is the west side of the east range of Old Court (1638–41) by master mason John Westley. Its focal point appears to be pure English Renaissance. Yet the passage through this gateway boasts a medieval-style fan vault ceiling, reminding us that unlike its European manifestation at the time, and despite this building's

architectural aplomb, the English Renaissance still sought security in a previous age. Clare College was founded in 1326 and was re-founded in 1338 by a granddaughter of Edward I, Elizabeth de Clare. Until 1856 it was known as Clare Hall. Looming beyond Old Court is King's College Chapel, the last pure manifestation of pre-Renaissance architecture in England. Its stonework was completed just 123 years before work began on Old Court.

The only changes to Old Court since the 1970s appear to be some minor alterations to the paths and evidence of additional foliage. The only other difference is the converging verticals, which have been corrected in the 'Then' image. Unless it is pointed out, it is easy to overlook this orthodoxy of architectural photography, based in the tradition of the 'picturesque'. Famous alumni include poet Siegfried Sassoon; DNA scientist James Watson; historian David Cannadine; Archbishop of Canterbury, Rowan Williams; benefactor Paul Mellon; and naturalist and broadcaster David Attenborough.

CLARE BRIDGE

The oldest surviving bridge in Cambridge

Left: Clare Bridge is the oldest bridge in Cambridge. It was built in 1638–40 by master mason Thomas Grumbold, at the same time as John Westley started building Old Court. Grumbold's son, Robert, may have been responsible for the giant pilasters, seen here on the west range of Clare College's Old Court. Taken in the 1950s by renowned photographer A.F Kersting, this view includes, from left to right, Fellows' Garden, Old Court west (commenced 1669), King's College Chapel and King's College Gibbs' Building. Such a viewpoint would be difficult to outshine anywhere in Cambridge – or Oxford for that matter. For scale and picturesque effect, Kersting has captured two men resting on the parapet as they admire the southern aspect of the Backs.

Above: The sense of timelessness, a fundamental ingredient in the beauty of the Backs, has been lovingly maintained. The only regrettable change is the replacement of the simple rammed-gravel pathway set against classical balustrading with this awkward combination of flags, cobblestones and a drainage channel. Perhaps 'Health and Safety' demanded it. The southern aspect of the Backs continues to be admired.

67

THE CAM, LOOKING SOUTH TO CLARE BRIDGE

Now a popular tourist destination for punting

Below: Looking south we see Thomas Grumbold's Clare Bridge with its characteristic sunken kinks to the balustrading. It is built in Ketton stone ashlar and is not only the oldest but the most elegant bridge over the Cam. Beyond is King's Bridge by William Wilkins (1819). This photograph by Edwin Smith was taken from Garret Hostel Bridge, almost certainly the present one, which was completed in 1960 and which helps date this harmonious image.

Right: As with most attractive places in the world, this stretch of the Cam has become a magnet for mass tourism within the last thirty years or so. Several companies offer trips, with some employees attired as if for the Venetian lagoon. It is perhaps more deserved here than anywhere else on earth to refer to eager tourists as punters.

SENATE HOUSE PASSAGE AND CAIUS COLLEGE'S GATE OF HONOUR

The Gate of Honour reflects the eclectic taste of the college's founder, John Caius

Senate House Passage runs between the back of Senate House and Gonville and Caius College, providing a convenient cut-through to Trinity Lane from the centre of Cambridge. In this 1950s photograph, a young member of Caius strolls through a sunlit Gate of Honour (1573–75) to reach Gonville and Caius College. To the left, a man watches passers-by as he rests on stone steps leading to Senate House.

The Gate of Honour is a curious architectural concoction, on a par with Hobson's Conduit (see page 8). It has the stylistic overload and scale of a grand memorial to a Roman merchant. The Gate of Honour is one of three commissioned by John Caius, re-founder of Caius College. The two others are the Gate of Humility (now in the Master's Garden) and the Gate of Virtue (between Tree and Caius courts). Caius' idea was that new students would enter his college by trudging under the Gate of Humility, pick up their step through the Gate of Virtue in their second year, and in their last year, stride through the Gate of Honour to collect their degrees from the Senate nearby. John Caius' gates are the earliest classical structures in Cambridge. Pevsner commented that they were not classically correct, although, to be fair, neither were many of the things the Romans themselves erected. Classically correct or not, the Gate of Honour is a brilliantly eccentric structure in design and in purpose.

THE GREAT GATE, TRINITY COLLEGE

Trinity has more Nobel laureates than any other Oxford or Cambridge college

Seen here in the late 1960s is the main entrance to Trinity College, the grandest college in Cambridge. The Great Gate was started in 1490 as part of King's Hall, one of the forerunners of Trinity. The name of Edward III is over the entrance because he was the monarch who granted Letters Patent to King's Hall. Great Gate was completed in 1528–35 during the reign of the founder of Trinity, Henry VIII. His uninspiring statue, seen here looking rather worse for wear, was put up in 1615. In its right hand is a chair leg instead of a sceptre, an undergraduate prank so old as to have become integral to this inept yet charming sculpture. Below the King's statue is the Royal Coat of Arms. Unlike other gatehouses in Cambridge, this one has a pedestrian entrance as well as a main entrance arch. Through these can be glimpsed part of Great Court, the largest in either Cambridge or Oxford.

Sometime in the intervening years the corner towers of the Great Gate have had their stonework cleaned or replaced. The statue of Henry VIII with its portcullis cover also seems to have been repaired and cleaned up. As in other parts of central Cambridge, cars have been banished and replaced with more tourists on foot, although bicycles are as popular as ever. Trinity College has more famous (and infamous) alumni and Nobel laureates than any other Cambridge college. Here is a small selection of alumni: poets Andrew Marvell, Lord Byron and Alfred Tennyson; philosophers Bertrand Russell and Ludwig Wittgenstein; writers William Thackeray, A.A. Milne, Lytton Strachey and Vladimir Nabokov; historians Thomas Macaulay and G.M. Trevelyan; composer Ralph Vaughan Williams; photographer William Fox-Talbot; sculptor Anthony Gormley; car and aeroplane pioneer Charles Rolls; journalists Vanessa Feltz and India Knight; film director Stephen Frears; Prime Ministers Earl Grey, Lord Melbourne, Stanley Baldwin and Jawaharlal Nehru; scientists Isaac Newton and Ernest Rutherford; spies Guy Burgess, Kim Philby and Anthony Blunt; royals Edward VII, George VI and Prince Charles.

THE WREN LIBRARY, TRINITY COLLEGE

One of the most magisterial buildings in Cambridge

Second only to King's College Chapel, Trinity College's library is the most magisterial building in Cambridge. Flanking the west side of Neville's Court, it was built in warm Ketton stone to Sir Christopher Wren's design in 1676–95 by master mason Robert Grumbold. Wren's first design with a cupola was rejected by the college, which must have been a little galling as he was undertaking the commission for nothing. However, the idea was not to be wasted. Nicholas Hawksmoor adapted it for Oxford's Radcliffe Camera. This photograph was taken in the 1940s and captures successfully the restrained facade with Wren's superimposed columns. The statues representing Divinity, Law, Physic (medicine) and Mathematics are by Gabriel Cibber, a favoured sculptor of Wren's.

Wren was a master at designing a pleasing visual effect while at the same time disguising a technical necessity. The hidden brick cone supporting the elegant dome of St Paul's Cathedral is a good example. Here he had three technical necessities: keeping the library's books free from damp, providing enough wall space for the book cases and supplying plenty of light. His solution was an open undercroft. This keeps the books well above ground level while providing ventilation for the floor on which they stand. The level of this floor lies at the horizontal line, just over half way up the grounded pillars; the point where the arches spring. The large windows on either side of the building provide the library with sufficient natural light for reading.

TRINITY COLLEGE CHAPEL AND ST JOHN'S COLLEGE

Trinity College Chapel was started in the reign of Queen Mary I and completed in the reign of Elizabeth I

From the left is the shadowed east end of Trinity College Chapel, followed by St John's College Gatehouse and, behind that, the tower of St John's College Chapel. The saloon car, parked behind the purposeful cyclist, is a Standard Vanguard dating this photograph to the mid 1950s. Trinity College Chapel, completed in 1567 in the reign of Protestant Elizabeth I, was started in 1555 at the initiative of Catholic Mary I and is one of the few buildings of her reign. Much of its material came from two religious foundations (Ramsey Abbey in Huntingdonshire and a Franciscan Friary where Sidney Sussex College now stands), which were demolished by her father Henry VIII as his contribution to the Reformation. Mary no doubt welcomed this example of recycling. St John's College Gatehouse, built in red brick, dates from 1511–20. Its heavy doors (1515) are mostly original. Above is the coat of arms of Lady Margaret Beaufort (d. 1509) whose will it was to found the college, which was enacted in 1511 by John Fisher, Bishop of Rochester. Above the Beaufort arms is a statue of St John the Evangelist. Behind the gatehouse is Sir George Gilbert Scott's huge chapel tower (1863–69), inspired by Pershore Abbey in Worcestershire.

The great east window of Trinity College Chapel can be seen more clearly in early morning sunlight. St John's Street (a continuation of Trinity Street) has been virtually pedestrianised. Although it wasn't part of his initial design, Sir George Gilbert Scott's chapel – the tallest and bulkiest building in Cambridge for many years – was considered to be overbearing. Since the completion of the much larger University Library building in 1934 (designed by Scott's grandson Giles Gilbert Scott), St John's chapel tower has come to be regarded as an integral part of the Cambridge skyline. Alumni of St John's include anti-slave trade campaigner William Wilberforce; poet William Wordsworth; discoverer of Neptune, John Couch Adams; astronomer John Herschel; anthropologist Louis Leakey; physicist and first splitter of the atom, Sir John Cockcroft; cosmologist Sir Fred Hoyle; discoverer of titanium, William Gregor; Prime Minister Lord Palmerston; runner Chris Brasher; cricketer Mike Brearley; authors Samuel Butler, Douglas Adams and Frederic Raphael; photographer Cecil Beaton; theatre director Jonathan Miller; journalist Andrew Gilligan; and actor Sir Derek Jacobi.

ST JOHN'S COLLEGE AND THE BRIDGE OF SIGHS

Queen Victoria's favourite spot in Cambridge

Above: St John's spans both sides of the Cam and boasts the largest contiguous set of buildings in central Cambridge. The Bridge of Sighs joins the two sides of the college, providing one of the most picturesque views in Cambridge. To the left is New Court (1826–31), built in Tudor Gothic style by Rickman and Hutchinson. To the right is the west range of Third Court (1669–72). Henry Hutchinson was the architect of the Bridge of Sighs, which was constructed in 1831 to connect the old part of St John's with the new. Queen Victoria must have been impressed, as she maintained that she loved this spot more than any other in Cambridge.

Right: St John's College was built throughout in brick when it was confined to the east of the Cam, but the decision to expand to the west in the early nineteenth century provided the opportunity to break with this tradition. The Gothic Revival made brick no longer fashionable. Part of the library (1623–28) can be seen peeping out at the distant end of the building on the right, complete with its date. The bridge, which is nothing like its namesake in Venice, has been a favourite spot for student pranks. Hanging a comical car from it – such as a pre-war Austin 7 or a post-war Reliant Robin, which had been lashed to a few punts and slipped under in the dead of night – became popular in the 1960s. The pièce de résistance, however, will always be the Austin 7 van placed on the roof of the Senate House in 1958.

HOLY SEPULCHRE (THE ROUND CHURCH)

One of only five surviving medieval English churches with a circular nave

Left: Where St John's Street meets Bridge Street, Holy Sepulchre (commonly called the Round Church) can be found. It was built in 1125–50, and is Romanesque; a fascinating crossover in the history of western architecture, where the medieval emerges from the classical. Maybe that is appropriate for the Round Church, for it stands where the winding medieval lane of St John's, Trinity Street and Trumpington Street meet the straight Roman road of Magdalene Street, Bridge Street and beyond. This 1940s photograph shows the church with its railings still intact. It is one of only five medieval English churches with a circular nave. Behind is the fifteenth-century north chapel with its nineteenth-century bell turret.

Above: Temple churches are usually associated with the Knights Templar or Knights of St John. This church is associated with neither; it was built by the little-known Fraternity of the Holy Sepulchre. In the fifteenth century the conical tower disappeared, but in 1841–43 the church was heavily restored by Anthony Salvin. Since the 'Then' photograph, the Victorian railings have sadly disappeared, although the north chapel and bell turret (minus its crenellations) have been cleaned. The usual street furniture has made its appearance, including a makeshift cycle stand, sufficiently lofty to secure a penny-farthing.

MAGDALENE BRIDGE AND THE QUAY

The river crossing that gave Cambridge its name

Left: Magdalene Bridge (formerly the Great Bridge) takes the old Roman road over the Cam at the place that gave the city its name. Thus, there has been a crossing here, on what is now Magdalene Street, since the road was first built. This latest version of the bridge was designed by Arthur Browne and completed in 1823. Magdalene Bridge is one of the earliest examples in Britain of a metal bridge with an arch built in three pins or sections, allowing it to flex under load. This view from the 1950s looks down towards St John's College, beyond the trees from which peeps the 'wedding cake tower' of New Court (1826–31). To the right, with steps leading down to the river from its grounds, is the corner of Magdalene College's First Court. This section was built around 1519 and it retains the same arrangement of medieval student rooms. (Details of its exterior alterations are given on page 87.)

Below: The ribbed, cast-iron structure of Magdalene Bridge was fully revealed when it was restored in 1982. The most striking change in this photograph is the number of immaculate punts now berthed in serried ranks to a landing stage, provided to service the explosion in tourism. Magdalene has abandoned its private access to the Cam at this point, perhaps because it now gets too crowded; a more believable explanation than the nineteenth-century jest about the then teetotal Magdalene College, which supposedly made it unnavigable here thanks to the volume of tea leaves tipped into the river. The buildings next to the bridge have eighteenth-century facades, but they conceal much older timber-framed structures beneath. Since the Then photograph these buildings have had a makeover, regrettably losing some of their chimney stacks in the process. Behind, where the large willow once grew, a new set of buildings has emerged. This is the Cripps Building (1963–67) by Powell and Moya.

RIVER CAM, LOOKING SOUTH FROM MAGDALENE BRIDGE

The Cripps Building was considered
a masterpiece by Pevsner

This bucolic sight, dating from the late 1940s, could
have been photographed in the middle of the
countryside, assuming they had punts there. It is
difficult to believe that it was taken from one of the
busiest bridges in Cambridge. Beyond the weeping
willow are the grounds of St John's College and the
confluence of the Cam with one of its tributaries,
the Bin Brook.

Today, the climbing roses and the attractive lamp have disappeared from the building to the right. But the biggest change to the view is the appearance of the Cripps Building. Here, in 1963–67, Powell and Moya provided for St John's College one of the largest modern developments in Cambridge. The Cripps Building bridges the Bin Brook and in so doing echoes Rickman and Hutchinson in 1821–31 when they built New Court, which Hutchinson joined to Third Court by his Bridge of Sighs. Pevsner thought the Cripps Building 'a masterpiece'. Beyond is the 'wedding cake tower' of New Court.

MAGDALENE STREET, LOOKING NORTH

Originally part of the Roman road that stretched from Colchester to Chester

Left: Magdalene Street – originally part of an old Roman road – runs into Castle Street and continues to Castle Hill. The Castle Hill area of Cambridge lies at what was the city's Roman town centre, then known as Duroliponte. The complete Roman road, which stretched from Colchester to Chester, was given the name Via Devana ('Chester Road') by the Cambridge geology professor Charles Mason. The name, coined around 1750, derives from the Roman for Chester: Deva. The lens used in this photograph from 1860 produces an interesting perspective: the giant impression made by the man to the left is emphasised by the diminutive size of the children walking hand-in-hand. Many of the buildings on the left are medieval structures, some with eighteenth-century facades. To the right is the main frontage of Magdalene College (c. 1585).

Above: Although the buildings to the left have been smartened up, the structural changes are surprisingly few since 1860. The major changes have all taken place opposite. Magdalene College's brick-built street frontage to First Court dates to around 1475. It has lost its original chimneys and some of its roofline behind, while the stucco – which was applied to First Court in 1759–60 and is apparent in the 1860 photograph – has been removed, revealing warm red brick. The extensive restoration of First Court was made by S. Dykes Bower in 1959–66. The building seen far right in the Then photo has been replaced by a pleasant open-grassed area, surrounded by railings and running down to the river. The south end of the fifteenth-century building has been remodelled, complete with an oriel window displaying Magdalene College's coat of arms.

THE PEPYS LIBRARY, MAGDALENE COLLEGE

Pepys's collection includes all six volumes of his diary

First called the New Building, the Pepys Library, here very soot-encrusted in the 1930s, took a long time to finish. This facade dates from 1679 and is thought to be by the scientist Robert Hooke, a friend of Sir Christopher Wren. Work on the building before it was designated a library could have started as early as 1587. It took at least until 1700 to complete, thanks to Magdalene College's impoverishment, perhaps provoked by one Benedict Spinola, a London banker who swindled them out of seven acres of real estate in Aldgate, London. The college didn't take its revenge on Mr Spinola until the 1980s when it included a very ugly gargoyle of him in its Quayside development. Samuel Pepys left his library to Magdalene (his old college) on his death in 1703. The date over the entrance (1724) tells when it was finally installed. The library, which has many treasures in addition to his famous diary, is arranged eccentrically by height of book rather than subject, in accordance with Pepys's instructions.

The Pepys Library has been thoroughly cleaned revealing its warm Ketton stonework. Whether the hanging baskets are required is a matter of taste. Magdalene was founded in 1428 as a hostel for monks studying at Cambridge. It was known as Buckingham College thanks to financial support from the 2nd and 3rd Dukes. As a monastic college it was dissolved by Henry VIII and straightaway re-founded in 1542 by Thomas Audley, one of the chief beneficiaries of the Dissolution. The college's name is pronounced, and indeed was originally spelt, Maudleyn. The full title, the College of St Mary Maudleyn, was given to it by Audley, ensuring as he did that his own name appeared within it. Henry Dunster, an alumnus, became the first President of Harvard, in the process introducing that title to the American colonies. He chose it because Harvard's appointed Master, Comenius, never turned up, and 'President' was the title of the Vice-Master at Magdalene. Thus, the designation for what was to become the most powerful job in the world can be traced back to here. In addition to Pepys and Dunster, famous alumni of Magdalene include mountaineer George Mallory; Irish nationalist Charles Stewart Parnell; actor Sir Michael Redgrave; writer C.S. Lewis; couturier of the Queen's outfits, Sir Norman Hartnell; BBC journalist John Simpson; film director Mike Newell; and TV presenter Katie Derham.

MAGDALENE STREET, LOOKING SOUTH

Magdalene Street was partially demolished and widened in 1912

This 1904 image records a time before the motorcar transformed our streets. Magdalene Street at this junction with Northampton Street (right) and Chesterton Lane (left) was far narrower than it is today. At the far left can be seen the chimneys of Magdalene College's First Court. Beyond and out of view is Magdalene Bridge.

Magdalene Street, Cambridge

The houses on the left, which were owned by Magdalene College, were demolished in 1912 to provide a hall for concerts and club meetings. The President (Vice-Master) of Magdalene responsible was Dr A.C. Benson, who, among his many other achievements, penned the words to 'Land of Hope and Glory'. The decision to demolish and widen the road was also probably influenced by the rapid increase in motorised traffic. Today people-powered vehicles are given precedence, evidenced here by the prominent markings on the road surface. Many of the buildings to the right are timber-framed and jettied, some dating back to medieval times, and most with numerous additions and subtractions since they were first constructed. In the eighteenth century it was popular to grace a much earlier building with a formal facade rather than demolishing and rebuilding. This provided architectural gravitas on the cheap. To the right is the Cambridge and County Folk Museum, housed in the former White Horse Inn, a sixteenth- and seventeenth-century building.

MAGDALENE STREET ENTRANCE TO BENSON COURT

Most of these buildings are owned
by Magdalene College

This photograph was taken some time before World
War II. Many of these buildings were once inns and
alehouses. The jettied building in the centre, as with
most along this street, had an internal timber frame
dating back to at least the sixteenth century. Those
Victorian favourites, bay windows, have been added
above and either side of the entrance to this post
office building. Of particular note are the carvings on
the gable ends above the first floor. These buildings
were owned by Magdalene College, whose entrance
is on the opposite side of the street.

From 1952 to 1958, the post office building, and those beyond, were converted for Magdalene College's use by David Roberts, an architect and former Fellow of the college. Gone were the days when a college would think nothing of knocking down a streetful of old houses to make way for a prestigious edifice. From 1925 until the 1970s Magdalene College used the area behind these buildings for expansion. Benson Court, Mallory Court and Buckingham Court all provided more facilities and further student accommodation. One of the entrances to this development, colloquially called Magdalene Village, is through the studded door seen in this photograph.

NORTHAMPTON STREET

These medieval timber-framed buildings have been subtly
remodelled throughout the twentieth century

Left: This 1920s photograph is of the corner of Northampton Street and Magdalene Street. This group of old properties is in dire need of repair. Three of the four are jettied, indicating their medieval timber framework. A customer has just bought a newspaper from the corner shop and appears to be walking towards his bicycle, propped against the kerb in an age when it was unnecessary for him to secure it from theft. The two women to the right wear the new post–World War I uniform of female emancipation: cloche hats and short skirts. They look fashionable and comfortably well off, and it is undoubtedly of and for them this photograph was taken.

Above: The newsagent has disappeared, a contemporary indicator of specialist shops becoming fewer and fewer. Its paintwork, not really a Cambridge light blue, is brighter than any paint that would have been applied to this building at any time in its long history. Pigments of this strength were not available until the 1960s. The other houses have been decorated more discreetly, although all have been restored. Their restorations provide instant history with the real past removed. Few would know that chimneys and doorways have disappeared or arrived. The large doorway has made an entrance with the confidence that it has always stood there. Where once the flappers posed, a jogger reminds us that a modern emancipation is fitness. The houses she runs past show that, for all the grandeur of its colleges, Cambridge is at heart a charming medieval market town of the type to be found throughout eastern England from the Humber to the English Channel.

CAMBRIDGE FROM CASTLE HILL

Originally the site of a Norman castle

Left: Looking over towards the city centre from Castle Hill, King's College Chapel can be seen on the misty horizon. To its right is the tower of St John's New Court. In 1859, when this photograph was taken, it really was new – just twenty-eight years old. In the foreground is the eleventh- to twelfth-century St Giles' Church, with what looks like a seventeenth- or eighteenth-century cupola. This photograph was taken in the year the chimes of Big Ben first rang out, inspired as it happens by those of Great St Mary's, Cambridge. But the event that had most resonance in the year this photograph was taken was caused by another Cambridge connection, Charles Darwin. Darwin's groundbreaking book *The Origin of Species* sold out on its first day of publication in 1859.

Below: Castle Hill is where Cambridge Castle, built shortly after the Norman Conquest, once stood. It is also the site of an earlier Roman camp. Today the county of Cambridgeshire is administered from County Hall on Castle Hill. Sadly, what was once a great view of the city is now obscured by the roof of St Giles', a capacious Victorian gothic church that replaced its predecessor in 1875. Its architects were T.F. and F. Healy. An arch from the original is incorporated, demonstrating succession in intent if not size. The Victorians excelled in ecclesiastical gargantuanism, such as the tower of Sir Gilbert Scott's St John's College Chapel, seen here to the left, which has dominated the skyline since 1869. On Ascension Day a hymn is sung from its top. Between Scott's tower and King's Chapel, the modest tower of the ancient parish church of St Mary the Great appears less great.

JESUS GREEN

Once used for grazing, this is now a popular and central park

Left: Jesus Green, a large open space now in the centre of Cambridge, has hosted many events over the centuries. Those events have ranged from the cruel – such as the burning of martyrs and witches in the sixteenth and seventeenth centuries – to the joyful, as shown in this photograph from 1911. Here, Second Lieutenant William Barnard Rhodes-Moorhouse (a former Trinity College student) makes a spectacular return to Cambridge by landing his Blériot Monoplane on Jesus Green. In March 1915 he was awarded the Victoria Cross posthumously for bombing Courtrai railway junction, a German troop hub.

Above: Jesus Green is still popular with those preferring to be airborne, especially skateboarders for whom this impressive bit of kit has been thoughtfully provided. Since 2001 the Cambridge Beer Festival, the longest running CAMRA (Campaign for Real Ale) festival, has been held on Jesus Green. Successful campaigns usually terminate when their ends have been achieved. This one, which started in 1974, hasn't.

JESUS COLLEGE GATEHOUSE

Jesus College started life as a nunnery
in the twelfth century

This is the entrance to Jesus College photographed in
the early 1950s. The passage to the gatehouse tower
is called 'The Chimney'. The tower was built by John
Alcock, Bishop of Ely and founder of the college,
in around 1500. Jesus College started life as a
nunnery in the 1130s, dedicated to the Virgin St Mary
and the Virgin St Radegund. By 1496, it had dwindled
to two nuns, one of whom had become pregnant. The
appalled, if in the circumstances amusingly named,
Bishop took this as an opportunity to close the
nunnery and turn it into a college. The building to the
left of the gate is early sixteenth century and until
1570 was used by the college for their grammar
school. Behind the left wall (1608–9) is the Fellows'
Garden. The building to the right, with its great
window, dates to the thirteenth century. Behind the
right wall (1681–82) is the Master's Garden. Height
was added to both buildings in 1718–20. Behind its
wrought iron gates and away from the city centre,
Jesus College exudes an air of peace and tranquillity.

Other than being replete with bicycles, the view is largely unchanged. Bishop Alcock's painted statue can now be seen more clearly over the gatehouse. Below and to the left of the statue is his coat of arms, three cock heads; to the right the arms of the Diocese of Ely. Trees have an important place in the college's history and its grounds have plenty of them, as glimpsed here. In his *Crazy Tales* of 1762, John Hall-Stevenson, having spent time studying under one of them, wrote:

Being of such a size and mass,
And growing in so wise a college,
I wonder how it came to pass
It was not called the Tree of Knowledge

Famous alumni include author of the Book of Common Prayer, Archbishop Thomas Cranmer; Astronomer Royal, Sir John Flamsteed; poet Samuel Taylor Coleridge; broadcaster Alistair Cooke; philosopher Roger Scruton; journalist Quentin Letts; playwright David Hare; author Nick Hornby; Prince Edward, Earl of Wessex; and Alexis Taylor, member of electro indie band Hot Chip.

SIDNEY SUSSEX
COLLEGE ENTRANCE

A Tudor Gothic Revival facade hides original Elizabethan buildings

Left: Founded in 1594, Sidney Sussex College occupies the site of a former Franciscan (Greyfriars) convent. The convent – alongside the other monastic foundations in England – was dissolved in 1538 by Henry VIII. The college is named after Lady Frances Sidney, wife of the Earl of Sussex, who established it under her will. This is the main entrance to the college from Sidney Street as it appeared in 1925. The architect was Sir Jeffry Wyattville who in 1821–32 more or less remodelled the whole college in the then fashionable Gothic Revival style, in this case the Tudor Gothic version. Beneath Wyattville's appended battlements, stepped gables and cement-as-stone sheathing, is the red brickwork of the original Elizabethan buildings constructed by Ralph Symonds in 1598.

Above: Wyattville's cement-as-stone has been repaired and cleaned. In colour the red brick chimneys hint at the building's Elizabethan foundations. Wyattville cannot be blamed entirely for his over-enthusiastic makeover. He gave the college the choice of either restoring their genuine Elizabethan buildings and erecting new ones as required, or this. They chose this. Famous alumni of Sidney Sussex include Lord Protector, Oliver Cromwell (in 1960 his head was buried under the college's anti-chapel in a secret location); politicians David Owen and Nick Raynsford (Raynsford was rusticated from Sidney Sussex for a year for hanging an anti-Vietnam war banner between the pinnacles of King's College Chapel); historian Asa Briggs; film director John Madden (*Shakespeare in Love*); novelist Nick Laird; journalist Andrew Rawnsley; and TV presenter Carol Vorderman.

CLOISTER COURT, SIDNEY SUSSEX COLLEGE

This impressive neo-Jacobean building has been beautifully preserved

The architect of Cloister Court, built in 1890–91, was the celebrated John Loughborough Pearson. The neo-Jacobean style he chose was unusual, as most of Pearson's works are Gothic Revival, which is exemplified by his masterwork Truro Cathedral. Since 1616 Sidney Sussex College had owned land that included an obscure fishing village on the windswept North East Lincolnshire coast. Its value and income increased enormously from 1873 when a railway was built connecting it to the burgeoning industrial towns of South Yorkshire and the East Midlands, such as Sheffield and Nottingham. Thus, Cloister Court was made possible by Wakes Week workers and their Cleethorpes landladies. This photograph was taken in 1914, the eve of World War I, when Cloister Court had stood for only twenty-three years.

Pearson's choice of red brick carries his Jacobean fantasy convincingly, especially its silhouette against the sky. Less convincing are his double-bow windows. They seem over-large, jammed-in and they compete for attention with the gable ends. However, the most challenging juxtaposition perhaps is the neo-Norman cloister with the neo-Jacobean facade. Yet in spite of these competing elements, Cloister Court impresses. In Britain, build quality, detailing and weather-resistance reached their apogee throughout the 30-year period before the outbreak of World War I. Pearson's contribution to Sidney Sussex College provides prime evidence of this.

SUSSEX STREET

Pevsner considered this the best piece of pre-war urban planning in Cambridge

Left: Sussex Street, which is off Sidney Street, was developed between 1928 and 1939 by Sidney Sussex College in a neo-Georgian style by E.R. Barrow. The street provides a thoughtfully designed complex of shops with student accommodation above. Architectural historian Pevsner praised Sussex Street as the 'best piece of pre-war urban planning at Cambridge'. This photograph was taken soon after the work was completed. The monument in the middle of the street serves as a lamppost and was added in 1932 when the street was widened.

Above: In 1991 the arch was added connecting both sides of the development and in 1992 Sussex Street was pedestrianised, providing a pleasant courtyard for student accommodation and commercial activity. It is only in the last twenty years or so that other universities in the UK have followed suit by providing both pursuits in one development. In too many cases they have produced less pleasing and sophisticated solutions than that delivered by E.R. Barrow, almost a lifetime ago.

MARKET HILL

A major distinction between Oxford and Cambridge

Left: If there is one important feature to distinguish Cambridge from Oxford, it is the main activity of a market town, conducted regularly in its centre. Here, customers search for fresh fruit and veg as they have done since Saxon times – well before the university arrived. In the background is Cambridge's Parish and University Church of St Mary the Great. To the right of St Mary's and further back is Waterhouse's tower for Caius College's Tree Court. Far right is a 1937 building in the popular ocean-liner style of the period by J. Murray Easton. It was commissioned by Caius College to contain college accommodation with ground-level shops. Immediately behind the market awning is a Gothic Revival fountain, built in 1856 to replace Hobson's Conduit (see page 8). Much of it was demolished in 1953 and its water ceased to flow in 1960. On several maps it is mysteriously designated a lavatory. This photograph was most likely taken in the early 1950s.

Below: If the Cambridge we see today started anywhere it would have been here. A river nearby, high enough to avoid flooding and with a Roman road just opposite, this had to be a good meeting place to buy and sell. Thus it became known as Market Hill, a misnomer anywhere else but in the Fens. At one time it was larger and L shaped, the street now called Pea's Hill being included. Today the market operates from Monday to Saturday with a flourishing farmer's market and arts and crafts fair on Sundays. Behind the awning are the remains of the Gothic Revival fountain.

PEAS HILL

John Mortlock's bank building has been open for borrowing and lending since 1783

Left: Once called Peasemarket Hill, some scholars believe its name can be traced back to it being a fish market (Pisces), although why Anglo-Saxon market traders would prefer to use a Latin descriptor is unclear. It may simply be where vegetables were once sold. At the far end of Peas Hill, on Bene't Street, is a branch of Barclays bank. This building had been used as a bank since 1783 when John Mortlock bought the site of an old friary and opened for business. He started by looking after the money of the Cambridge well-to-do so that they didn't have to carry their cash to London and risk being robbed in the process. Far right is the east end of St Edward King & Martyr Church with its large east window (1858–60) by Sir George Gilbert Scott. Dedicated to Edward the Confessor, the last Anglo-Saxon King of England (1043–66), this building dates back to the twelfth century. A Saxon coffin-stone was excavated on the site twenty or so years before this charming 1930 photograph was taken.

Above: In the intervening years three buildings have disappeared to be replaced by a large residential block with shops at ground level. The bank, which is still a branch of Barclays, has gained some new dormers. St Edward's stonework has been cleaned and restored. To park a car here you must exhibit an approved disabled badge and not outstay your allotted time. The city's stringent parking rules, assuming the visitor can find somewhere to park, are to be ignored at the visitor's peril.

PEAS HILL AND
WHEELER STREET

Changes continue to take place at this city-centre crossroads

Left: The demolition of several timber-framed, wattle-and-daub buildings progresses in this 1904 photograph, despite the 'Business as Usual' posters. They were to make way for an extension to the Cambridge Free Library. The library's delicate dome, built in the 1890s, can be seen through the skeletal remains of the buildings. Behind the dome is the main hall of the Guildhall. The onlookers appear to be waiting for something spectacular to happen – a forced eviction perhaps? We can but guess.

Below: The Free Library now houses the Tourist Information Centre where the dome can still be appreciated from within. The hall of the Guildhall has lost its chimneys. Far left is the rear of the main new arrival – a vast neo-Georgian Guildhall built in 1936–37 by C. Cowles Voysey. It faces Market Hill. Opposite the former library, on the right-hand side of Wheeler Street, is the Corn Exchange building by R.R. Rowe (1874). In the distance, and dominating the horizon, is the roof of the Lion Yard Shopping Centre (1970), the first development of its scale in Cambridge. It takes its name from the Red Lion Inn and its coaching yard, which once stood on a relatively small part of this site.

PETTY CURY

Possibly named for the 'little cooks' that worked here

Left: At one time there were bakers' stalls here, where Petty Cury joins Market Hill to Sidney Street. In his famous diary, Samuel Pepys writes that the street's name might have derived from 'petit cury' or 'little cooks' row'. The Burton's shop window is quite intriguing, juxtaposing mannequins with real people, reflections of shop fronts with real ones and showing us that a man's suit could be bought for 37/- (£1.85) in the 1930s. To the left and behind the turreted building can be seen a finer turret. It belongs to King's College Chapel.

Above: Petty Cury is now pedestrianised and Burton's has become an opticians. The shop-front has been remodelled to appear older than it actually is. The plain brick building on the left will have been erected long after the previous photograph was taken. The turreted building has been rendered and is now brilliant white – a paint pigment that only became extensively available in the 1960s. Inevitably, hanging flower baskets have appeared throughout the scene. The grandeur of King's College Chapel still rises above these trifling differences.

ST ANDREW'S STREET
AND CHRIST'S COLLEGE

Alumni of Christ's College include John Milton, Charles Darwin
and the current Archbishop of Canterbury, Rowan Williams

Left: This photograph was taken in 1920, just two years after the 'war to end all
wars' had ended. Many Cambridge students had joined up as subalterns, and of
these a sizeable proportion never returned having been killed or maimed, often
when leading men 'over the top'. The Cambridge we see here must have felt
strange for those who did return. To the left in this photograph is St Andrew the
Great. Although the church's history reaches back to the eleventh century there
are few remains of the original building. The church was rebuilt in late Gothic style
by Ambrose Poynter and dates to 1842–43. Inside is a memorial to Captain Cook
and his family – three of whom are buried here. To the left is the clock tower of
Foster's Bank by Alfred Waterhouse (1890–93); to the right is the sooty facade of
Christ's College. Christ's College was founded as God's House in 1437 where
King's College Chapel now stands, moving to this site in 1448. In 1505 it was
re-founded as Christ's College by Lady Margaret Beaufort. First Court and its
turreted gatehouse (1505–11) were built in brick and then refaced with Ketton
stone by James Essex in the 1760s.

Below: Stonework has been cleaned on either side of the road but a major change
is the disappearance of the building behind St Andrew's, replaced by the entrance
to the Lion Yard shopping centre (1970), part of which can be seen to the left.
Another change has occurred at the end of the street. The imposing corner shop
has been replaced by a newer building (a branch of Lloyds Bank) that appears to
be older, at least superficially, than its predecessor. Famous alumni of Christ's
College include poet John Milton; scientist Charles Darwin; South African soldier
and statesman, Jan Smuts; last Viceroy of India, Lord Mountbatten; writer C.P.
Snow; sculptor Sir Anthony Caro; historian Simon Schama; Archbishop of
Canterbury and theologian, Rowan Williams; TV presenter Richard Whiteley; and
comedian Sacha Baron Cohen.

ST ANDREW'S STREET, LOOKING SOUTH

A prime retail spot since 1840

The aptly named Sayle department store was founded by Robert Sayle in 1840 when he bought a small drapery shop on this site. He had the novel idea of displaying the price on each of the goods for sale in the window, refusing to haggle or accept payment on account, which was normal practice at the time. Instead, he took smaller fixed margins on more items. As his business grew it took in a brewery and even an undertaking service. The different styles of the buildings, each handsomely designed, indicate the success of Robert Sayle's department store when this photograph was taken in 1900.

Robert Sayle's department store became part of the John Lewis Partnership in 1940. In 2008, spearheaded by John Lewis, a large area behind these well-restored facades (which connected to the existing Lion's Yard shopping centre) was launched as the Grand Arcade. It has over fifty shops and cafes. Part of the development is the Grand Arcade Cycle Park, the first dedicated cycle park connected to a shopping mall in the country with 500 parking places and a cycle shop. It was encouraged by the removal of cycle parking facilities from the centre of Cambridge. Also included in the Grand Arcade development is the Public Library and Cambridge Magistrates' Court (far right). Under the canopy on the left is the St Andrew's Street entrance to the Grand Arcade.

YE OLD CASTEL HOTEL /
THE REGAL CINEMA

There has been a drinking establishment on this site since the thirteenth century

Left: In 1905, a woman wearing a large hat cycles past Ye Old Castel Hotel on St Andrew's Street. To the left is St Andrew's Baptist Church, completed only two years earlier by G. and R.P. Baines. The Castel was established before 1243 making it one of the oldest inns in Cambridge. It was reconstructed in 1620 and enlarged in 1891, stretching almost as far as the church.

Below: The Castel burnt down in 1934 and in 1937 the Regal Cinema opened in its place. From 1972 to 1997 it operated as a two-screen cinema. It was then bought by the Wetherspoon chain which converted the ground floor into a large pub in 1999. The three-screen Arts Picture House took over the rest of the building. Today, a woman wearing a more protective style of head covering cycles towards the Castel's much-reduced neighbour, the Castle, which since 1999 has been competing as best it can with its ubiquitous pub-chain neighbour. St Andrew's, now minus its spire, is still going strong and features a coffee shop for interested visitors.

DOWNING COLLEGE

The grand scale and open spaces of Downing College
give it the look and feel of an American university

Downing College was founded in 1800 from the proceeds of the will of Sir George Downing. Downing was the grandson and namesake of the builder of 10 Downing Street and great-grandson of Emmanuel Downing, one of the founders of Massachusetts. The American connection is better evidenced by the college's Greek Revival style, which is unlike that of any other Cambridge college and preempts Thomas Jefferson's influential University of Virginia by ten years. With its sense of space and grandeur, Downing looks and feels like the campus of an American university. William Wilkins was the original architect and his original buildings (1807–12), although not copied slavishly, have influenced its development. This 1950s photograph shows the magnificent north and east ranges (1929–32) by Sir Herbert Baker. These grand buildings were made possible by the bequest of Sidney Wynn Graystone, a Downing College alumnus. At the end of the path is a comparatively humble Regent Street.

An attractive avenue of huge trees now flanks the path running in front of the Graystone buildings, hence this photo being taken further to the left. The lantern of the Maitland Robinson Library (left) now peeps above the east of the range. The library, designed by architect Quinlan Terry and built in Ketton ashlar stone, was completed in 1993. Downing's famous alumni include literary critic F.R. Leavis, film director Michael Apted, film director and restaurant critic Michael Winner, theatre director Trevor Nunn, writer Howard Jacobson, writer and illustrator Quentin Blake, cricketer Mike Atherton and comedian John Cleese.

SELWYN COLLEGE

Originally established to educate the sons of clergymen

Left: Selwyn College was founded by subscription in 1882, in honour of George Selwyn, first Bishop of New Zealand. Its charter stated that it should 'make provision for those who intend to serve as missionaries overseas and... educate the sons of clergymen'. An unstated impetus for its foundation was the repeal of the Universities Tests Act in 1871, which meant that non-conformists and even non-Christians could now take up fellowships at the Universities of Oxford, Cambridge and Durham. This 1911 photograph shows Selwyn's Dining Hall (to the right), which was completed by Grayson and Ould in 1909. Left is Selwyn's Chapel (1893–95) by Sir Arthur Blomfield with windows by the celebrated Victorian stained-glass designer Charles Eamer Kempe. As can be seen from its silhouette, Blomfield was inspired by King's better-known chapel. That a deliberate decision was taken to build a chapel before a dining hall is unsurprising given Selwyn's objectives.

Above: With its lofty redbrick neo-Tudor buildings set amidst expansive green lawns, Selwyn looks decidedly better in colour. Here some repair work is being undertaken on the dining hall in anticipation of the arrival of a new batch of students. Selwyn was only granted full collegiate status in 1958, yet in recent years it has appeared top or consistently near the top in the *Independent's* Tompkins Tables, which ranks colleges in Cambridge in order of their undergraduate performance in that year's examinations. Famous alumni of Selwyn include journalist Malcolm Muggeridge, Bishop Richard Harries, Archbishop John Sentamu, broadcaster Clive Anderson, writer Robert Harris, and actors Thandie Newton, Hugh Laurie and Tom Hollander.

NEWNHAM COLLEGE

Newnham's alumni includes Margaret Drabble, A.S. Byatt and Iris Murdoch

Below: Newnham College was founded in 1871, mainly at the instigation of philosopher, liberal educator and supporter of women's rights, Henry Sidgwick. Its co-founder was Millicent Garrett Fawcett. Newnham's first Principal, Miss Clough, and her successor, Mrs Sidgwick, set the tone, ensuring that Newnham and its students had a more liberal and independent outlook than that encouraged by Cambridge's only other women's college, Girton. It moved from a rented house on Regent Street to its present site in Newnham Village, now enveloped by Cambridge, in 1875. The college's neo-Queen Anne style buildings are by Basil Champneys. Seen here in 1890 is the two-year-old Clough Hall.

Right: Newnham is still a women-only college and continues to attract students holding liberal and independent views. Given the fact that it is a relative newcomer in Cambridge its list of famous alumni is extraordinary by any standard. They include politicians Diane Abbot and Patricia Hewitt; actors Eleanor Bron and Emma Thompson; academics Germaine Greer and Mary Beard; TV presenters Joan Bakewell, Claire Balding and Sarah Dunant; rabbi and broadcaster Julia Neuberger; psychologist Penelope Leach; poet Sylvia Plath; cookery pundit Jane Grigson; BBC director Patricia Hodgson; Vice Chancellor of Cambridge University, Alison Richard; and writers Margaret Drabble, A.S. Byatt, Iris Murdoch, Katharine Whitehorn and Claire Tomalin.

THE OLD GLOBE INN, HILLS ROAD

While mock funerals have long gone, these premises continue
to please their discerning customers

Left: Hills Road runs more or less straight south as a continuation of St Andrew's Street and Regent Street, passing Station Road on its way. Here, in 1910, a mock funeral procession passes the Globe public house on its way to the railway station. Mock funeral processions were often assembled in the later nineteenth and early twentieth century by undergraduates to grace any one of their number who had been sent down (i.e. dismissed from the university for a serious offence). These comic celebrations caused some embarrassment for the university, as the individual in question made his very public and unabashed exit. One incentive for an earlier mock funeral procession may have been the opening of Cambridge Railway Station in 1845. The university was horrified sufficiently to ban its students from using it.

Below: In 2010 the old Globe changed its name. Those who know that Hills Road follows the Roman Via Devana (see page 87) may assume its new name has something to do with that but they would be entirely wrong. The current proprietor, who already owned the successful Empress in Romsey Town, Cambridge, was inspired by a nearby cluster of street names (Cyprus, Hobart, Madras, Malta, Suez) built in 1885–95, at the height of the British Empire. At the 2010 CAMRA Cambridge Beer Festival the Empress won the Pub of the Year award, so celebrations may yet return to Hills Road.

HOMERTON COLLEGE

Students form living sculptures in these photographs by the author

Homerton College can trace its ancestry back to Homerton in Hackney, London, where it began as a Congregational society training 'young men for the Christian ministry'. It moved to Cambridge in 1894 taking over the defunct Cavendish College, which had been set up to provide an education for poor male students to sit the Cambridge Tripos (BA Honours examinations) but which had failed through lack of funding. On moving to Cambridge, the college became a women-only institution and then a teacher-training college with a national reputation under Mary Miller Allen, Principal from 1903 to 1935. Men were readmitted in the 1970s and the college became an 'Approved Society of the University' in 1976. Students have arranged themselves into an 'S' shape for this photo set up by the author (and former Homerton Sculpture lecturer) in 1973. The students agreed to become part of this visual pun sculpture as a parting gift to their lecturer.

In 2001 Homerton started to accept students for full Cambridge University degrees in a range of subjects besides teacher-training. Today Homerton has 1,200 students, more than any other college at Cambridge. Homerton's application for full Cambridge University status was accepted in 2008 and completed by Royal Charter in March 2010. In the background of this photograph are Homerton's core buildings, including the Great Hall, which was designed in a red-brick neo-Tudor style. They have weathered well since they were built in 1876–89 for Cavendish College by architects Giles and Gough. To mark Homerton's new status, in 2009 the Students Union agreed to form themselves into a large letter 'A', thus completing the sculpture in the 'Then' photograph. When combined, the two photographs spell 'SA' (examples of which are being waved here). Famous alumni of Homerton include actress and singer Julie Covington; actors Olivia Colman, Dan McSherry, Cherie Lunghi and Tamzin Merchant; comedians and TV presenters Sandi Toksvig and Nick Hancock; and Head Master of Eton College, Tony Little.

CHURCHILL COLLEGE

Built as a memorial to Sir Winston Churchill

Left: Churchill College was built between 1959 and 1968 by architects Richard Sheppard, Robson & Partners, and Stirling & Gowan. It was built as a memorial to Sir Winston Churchill, with the intention that it should focus on the sciences – a puzzling decision given the great Englishman's known strengths. A possible link, perhaps, is Churchill's love of building brick walls. There are certainly plenty of them here. Warm, brown Staffordshire is the brick of choice. The college is designed around the idea of cloisters, with seven larger grassed courts and three smaller concrete-paved ones. This photograph was taken just after the college had been completed.

Right: The brickwork has weathered well and its warmth can be fully appreciated in this colour photograph. Using these bricks provides an English adaptation of European modernism, lending these courts a more human dimension, which is enhanced again by the mature trees. As expected, Health and Safety balustrades have made their inevitable appearance in the intervening years. Thankfully, a focus on science and technology did not rule for long, as evidenced in Churchill College's famous alumni, which includes broadcaster, writer and former Rector of the Royal College of Art, Sir Christopher Frayling; physicist and Lucasian Professor of Mathematics at Cambridge, Michael Green; broadcaster and Professor of the History of the Church at Oxford, Diarmaid MacCulloch; inventor of the Internet search engine Alta Vista, Michael Burrows; and founder of independent record label Rough Trade, Geoff Travis.

NEW HALL / MURRAY EDWARDS COLLEGE

Designed by Chamberlin, Powell and Bon, architects of the Barbican Centre

New Hall for women students started life with sixteen undergraduates at a house in Silver Street in 1954, when Cambridge had the highest proportion of men of any university in the United Kingdom. It moved to its present site in 1964. The college's new buildings, designed by Chamberlin, Powell and Bon, were completed between 1962 and 1966. This impressive picture shows a segment of the ferro-concrete dome being lifted into place. The size and weight of each section was finely calculated with regard to the lifting capacity of the crane. This was the first time anything of this scale, design and material had been built in England.

The bold design of these buildings is now set against some of the most delightful gardens in any of Cambridge's colleges. From the interior, Chamberlin, Powell and Bon's dome appears to float over the largest dining hall in the university – a result of light being brought in through windows seen here but hidden from the diners. The effect of the dome's levitation over one's head is echoed at one's feet. The centre of the floor is an extensive well-disguised section on which food, and indeed any other form of entertainment, can rise genie-like into the centre of celebrations. At each corner of the structure is a half-domed staircase tower. Chamberlin, Powell and Bon, who have more listed buildings than any other post-war architectural practice, also designed the huge Barbican development in the City of London. Like the Barbican, New Hall conveys a sense of modernist grandeur infused with creativity. Still a women-only college, New Hall is now named Murray Edwards College in honour of its first President, Dame Rosemary Murray and alumna Ros Edwards who gave the college a £30 million donation. Other famous alumni include TV presenters Mishal Husain and Claudia Winkleman; comedienne Sue Perkins; Warden of Merton College Oxford, Dame Jessica Rawson; Director of Oxfam, Dame Barbara Stocking; novelist Frances Vernon; and actor and Oscar winner, Tilda Swinton.

GIRTON COLLEGE GATEHOUSE

The first women-only college at Cambridge

Girton was the first all-women college at Cambridge. It is situated two miles outside Cambridge in the village of Girton, from which it takes its name. Its safe distance from the other colleges would have helped avoid enraging influential conservative members of the university and, at the same time, discouraged embarrassing visits from male undergraduates. Girton was founded in 1869 by educational pioneers Emily Davies and Barbara Leigh Smith Bodichon, supported by liberal-minded male members of the university. Originally named the College for Women, it was at first situated at an even safer distance from Cambridge – Hitchin in Hertfordshire. It moved to its present site in 1873. Seen here in 1929 is Girton's formidable gatehouse. It was built in 1887 in a neo-Tudor Gothic style. Its architect was Paul Waterhouse, son of Alfred Waterhouse who built Girton's Old Wing.

In 1948 Girton became a full member of Cambridge University. In 1977 the first male Fellows arrived and in 1979 the first male undergraduates. The only prominent difference between this photograph and the older one is the modern car. The rich red brick of the gatehouse has stood the test of time. Over the years, Girton has built a formidable academic reputation. Its famous alumni includes founder of the *Huffington Post*, Ariana Huffington; conductor Sister Mary Berry; authors Sally Beauman and Rosamond Lehmann (whose novel *Dusty Answer* was based on her time at Girton); comedians and TV presenters Sandi Toksvig and Dr Phil Redmond; Queen Margrethe II of Denmark; Supreme Court Judge, Baroness Brenda Hale; President of the International Court of Justice, Rosalyn Higgins; and many distinguished scientists and mathematicians.

COTTENHAM

This pretty Fenland village is now part of Cambridge's commuter belt

Although it could be reached by six miles of dry land from Cambridge, the village of Cottenham lay at the very edge of the wetland Fens. Before they were drained in the nineteenth century, there were waterlogged marshes all the way from Cottenham to Ely, some twenty miles away. The tower of All Saints' Church is over 30 metres high and stands as a beacon overlooking the Cambridgeshire Fens. A church has been here since Saxon times, although this one dates mostly from the fourteenth and fifteenth centuries. The upper part of its tower blew down in an early seventeenth-century gale, unsurprising in this windy part of England, and was rebuilt in 1617–19. The ogee-shaped pinnacles bear a distant resemblance to those of King's College Chapel. In this photograph from 1900, ladies of the village gather to celebrate the Relief of Mafeking in the Boer War. Perhaps they are planning to cycle to Cambridge for the main festivities.

Like every pretty village near a city, over the last thirty years Cottenham has boomed as a commuter dormitory for Cambridge. Here in the High Street, replacement windows and doors say as much about early twenty-first century life in England as the commendable attempt at recycling. The thatched cottage is reputed to have once been the family home of John Coolidge, baptised here in 1604. He emigrated to New England and among his descendants is the thirtieth President of the United States, Calvin Coolidge. A charming sundial painted on the tower of the church (left) shows the time of the day this photograph was taken. Although its advice may be discomforting, it is rather apt for this book.

GRANTCHESTER

Immortalised in the poetry of Rupert Brooke

The village of Grantchester lies just south of Cambridge on the River Cam. It has always been a popular destination for students visiting by foot, as well as by punt (which was introduced in the latter half of the nineteenth century). The poet Rupert Brooke lodged with the owner of the village's Orchard Tea Garden in 1909 and at the Old Vicarage in 1911. He immortalised the pleasant journey to Grantchester, its church and its tea garden in his poem to homesickness ('The Old Vicarage, Grantchester') penned in the Café des Westens, Berlin, in May 1912. Four lines will suffice:

Ah God! To see the branches stir
Across the moon at Grantchester!...
Stands the Church clock at ten to three?
And is there honey still for tea?

Brooke died in 1915 of septicaemia in a French hospital ship in the Aegean. Churchill, then First Sea Lord, telegrammed a relative to attend Brooke's funeral in Skyros on his behalf with the encouragement, 'We shall not see his like again. WSC.' This photograph was taken in 1929 when Brooke was still a celebrated household name.

Grantchester continues to attract visitors from all over the world, especially to the church of St Andrew & St Mary, which has a very good fourteenth-century chancel and Decorated Gothic windows. The name of Rupert Brooke is commemorated in the church, in the name of a pub and in the Orchard Tea Garden. Grantchester is said to have more Nobel Prize winners and world-class academic residents than any other village. The churchyard also contains many distinguished names. On a lighter note, a well-known song by Pink Floyd, whose members came from Cambridge, is called 'Grantchester Meadows'.

STRAWBERRY FRUIT PICKERS / CAMBRIDGE SCIENCE PARK

From farmland to 'Silicon Fen'

Left: Cambridge was, until the late twentieth century, surrounded by farmland. There were also a few military airfields, such as Duxford, which is now part of the Imperial War Museum. There is still much uninterrupted and well-cultivated farmland as the soil here is amongst the most productive in the country. In this 1910 photograph a host of fruit-pickers are being brought by horse-drawn charabanc from Cambridge and elsewhere to get the crop in before it 'goes over'.

Above: Cambridge Science Park owes its origins to Trinity College Cambridge, which has owned the land on which it is built since the college's foundation by Henry VIII. By 1970, part of this land – which had been used in World War II by the US Army to prepare tanks and other vehicles for D Day – had been standing derelict for over twenty years. Trinity College decided to draw up plans to develop it as a park for emerging science and technology enterprises, many of which could be connected with the University of Cambridge for research and development purposes. The plan, the first in the UK, took inspiration from the relationship between Stanford University, California, and what came to be known as 'Silicon Valley'. As Cambridge's Science Park developed, the media inevitably began to call it 'Silicon Fen'.

INDEX